A Southern View of the Invasion of the Southern States and War of 1861-65

Samuel A'Court Ashe

All rights reserved. No part of this publication may be reproduced, without the prior permission of the copyright owner. The views and ideas expressed in this book are the personal option of the author, and don't necessarily represent the views of the Publisher.

© Copyright 1980 by Snowball Publishing

www.snowballpublishing.com

info@snowballpublishing.com

Contents

Preface...5

The States..5

1. The Slave Trade..7
2. Steps Leading to War 10
3. Nullification, North and South 19
4. The States Made the Union 25
5. Nullification, North and South 31
6. Ratification of the Constitution by Virginia, New York, and Rhode Island...34
7. Secession, Insurrection of the Negroes, and Northern Incendiarism 37
8. The Modern Case of John Brown 51
9. Why South Carolina Seceded 54
10. Secession of the Cotton States 60
11. President Lincoln's Inaugural...65
12. Lincoln and the Constitution 67
13. Lincoln the Lawyer 75
14. Lincoln's Inhumanity 78
15. Lincoln the Usurper 82
16. Abraham Lincoln, the Citizen 86
17. Lincoln the Strategist 91
18. Conditions Just After the War 93
19. The War Between the Northern States and the Southern States..97
20. Speech of Jefferson Davis at Mississippi City, Mississippi in 1888 100

...

Preface

The States

Originally there was no connection between the settlements along the coast. In 1776 they held a meeting and declared their separation from England and asserted that each State was a free, independent and sovereign State; and by a treaty of peace, that was admitted by England.

In 1781 the States entered into a confederacy and again declared the independence and sovereignty of each State. In 1788 a union was proposed to go into effect between any nine States that ratified the Constitution. Eleven States ratified the Constitution and it went into operation between them. George Washington was elected President of the eleven States.

In ratifying that Constitution Virginia and New York particularly affirmed that the people of any State had a right to withdraw from the Union, and there was general assent to that claim, and it was taught in the text book at West Point.

There arose at various times differences between the Southern States and the Northern States but all these were peaceably settled except as to African slavery.

For some cause South Carolina seceded in December, 1860, and presently was joined by six other Southern States. Neither Congress nor the President took any action against these States. But at length Congress passed a measure proposing that the States should amend the Constitution and prohibit Congress from interfering with Negro slavery in any State, with the expectation that such an amendment would lead the seceded States to return.

Presently the new President was led to deny the right of a State to withdraw from the Union, and he started a war against the seceded States and called on the other States to furnish troops for his war. When North Carolina and Virginia and other Southern States were called on to furnish troops to fight the seceded States, North Carolina said, "You can get no soldiers from this State to fight your unholy war," and North Carolina withdrew from the Union and so did Virginia and two other States.

Then the Supreme Court in a case before it declared that under the Constitution the President had no right to make war and the Constitution did not give Congress the right to make war on any State.

So, it mentioned the war as one between the Northern and Southern States and said the right of the matter in dispute was to be determined by the "wager of battle," thus ignoring the light and justice of the claim in dispute. And so the Northern States conquered those that had seceded.

1. The Slave Trade

In the Library of the State College at Raleigh, N.C., there is a notable book of some three hundred and fifty pages and forty-nine illustrations—the fifteenth publication of the Marine Research Society, of Salem, Mass., and published in Vermont—the title being: Slave Ships and Slaving.

The introduction was written by a British Navy Officer, and the text is by George F. Dow. Within ten years after the discovery of America the Spaniards began to transport Africans to work in their possessions, and all the maritime nations of Europe followed their example; and during the next two hundred and fifty years the English transported twice as many as all other countries put together.

They began in Queen Elizabeth's time, kept it up in the next reign, and, in 1662, the Duke of York undertook to transport to the British colonies three thousand slaves every year. Ten years later the King himself became interested and, under contract, England got from Spain the exclusive right to supply the Spanish colonies; and the King of England and the King of Spain each received one-fourth of the profits.

Between 1680-88 England had two hundred and forty-nine slave ships; from 1713, for twenty years, 15,000 slaves were annually brought to America. In 1786, England brought over 97,000 slaves. During eleven years, 1783-93, Liverpool owned eight hundred and seventy-eight vessels in this trade, and imported many thousands of slaves in the West Indies. They were worth some 15,000,000 pounds of that period.

While Liverpool was the chief port for this trade, Bristol was a close second. Then, over here, New England was not slow. Massachusetts started in 1638. However, Rhode Island became the rival of Liverpool.

Ten pages of this volume are devoted to the operations in Rhode Island. There nearly everyone was interested. In 1750, "Rum was the chief manufacture of New England." About 15,000 hogsheads of molasses were annually converted into mm in Massachusetts alone. The number of stills in operation was almost beyond belief. In Newport there were no less than twenty-two.

With mm they purchased Negroes in Africa; these were exchanged for molasses in the Caribbean Islands and South America, and the molasses was brought to the New England stills; and so the profitable business was carried on in a circle to an extent beyond ordinary imagination! It was the very basis of New England's prosperity.

At Newport, Bristol, and Providence, some of the most respectable and wealthy merchants were engaged in the trade. Even preachers and philanthropists were advocates. "One elder, whose ventures in slaving had usually turned out well, always returned thanks on the Sunday following the arrival of a slaver that the Africans could enjoy the blessing of a Gospel dispensation."

The Southern colonies had no ships, nor any molasses. They were not in the trade. However, the British Slaving Company, in which the King of England was partner, was in duty bound to supply the needs of the colonies, as particularly required by Good Queen Anne. The Colonies were forbidden to manufacture, and their products were required to be shipped to England, where they were exchanged for British goods. So, the more slaves making products, the more good the Colonies bought in England.

At length Virginia forbade any more importation but the King annulled that Virginia law. In Jefferson's draught of the Declaration of Independence he denounced the King most severely for annulling these prohibitions. However, in 1774, importations were forbidden by the people of North and South Carolina, and there were no importations until 1803, when South Carolina opened her port for four years.

Great Britain abolished the trade in 1807, just as the Congress of the United States did. After a few years, other countries followed our example: Spain in 1820; Portugal in 1830; the trade between Portuguese Africa and Brazil did not cease until Brazil, in 1888, put a stop to it.

The Southern Colonies had no ships engaged in this trade, nor any molasses or rum, but, as the matter worked out, those States were the greatest sufferers in the end. Since 1800, the labor of Africans at the South has largely supplied the world with cotton.

That this volume has been prepared by the Marine Research Society, of Salem, Mass., speaks well for New England, and it should be in every library of the South.

2. Steps Leading to War

During the Revolutionary War there had been a joining of hearts and hands to secure the independence of the several colonies, and at length, in 1783, Great Britain declared each colony by name to be a free, independent and sovereign State. These States had entered into a Confederacy, and later a change was proposed to go into effect between any nine of them that agreed. Eleven ratified the new Constitution, the other two then becoming foreign States.

At that time there was slavery, in all the States except Massachusetts, and every State recognized the right of every other State to have slavery. Indeed, the Constitution prohibited the Congress from forbidding the introduction of slaves for twenty years, and required that if any slave escaped from his owner, he was to be returned to his master.

In time, for one reason or another, the opposition to slavery grew and grew, but the Constitution remained unchanged. The number of slave States was equal to that of free States, and as the States were equal in the Senate, the conflicting views balanced.

Then, in 1820, when Missouri and Maine wanted to become States, a compromise was agreed on; when a slave State was admitted, a Free State also was to be admitted; and north of the Missouri line should be free territory, and south of it slavery might be established by the people.

Year by year the anti-slavery sentiment increased. There had been but two political parties, the Whigs and the Democrats. But, at length in August, 1843, the Liberty Party was formed at the North. It declared that "the moral laws of the Creator are paramount to all human laws," and "we ought to obey God rather than man."

Five years later, in 1848, another party was organized, called the Free-Soil Party. And now a great campaign was made at the North against slavery. At the election, thirteen Free Soilers were elected to Congress, and when Congress met, the slavery question came up. Some of the States had refused to observe the Constitution, so it was proposed that Congress should pass a law requiring the Federal Courts to obey the Constitution about returning slaves to their owners. In advocating this law, Daniel Webster, the great Senator from Massachusetts said, in his speech in the Senate, that "there was unusual feeling at the North created by an incessant action on the public mind of Abolition societies, Abolition presses and Abolition lectures." Says he: "No drum-head in the longest day's march was ever more incessantly beaten and smitten than public sentiment at the North had been, every month and day and hour, by the din and rub-a-dub of Abolition workers and Abolition preachers."

And, on March 11, 1850, in the Senate, Seward declared: "There is a higher law than the

Constitution," etc., etc. And now all the Abolition leaders became Ambassadors of the Deity to enforce His Higher Law. And so Congress passed the Fugitive Slave Law.

In the midst of the din described by Daniel Webster, Mrs. Harriet Beecher Stowe wrote the story of Uncle Tom's Cabin in which she depicted the life of a slave as so miserable as to arouse the utmost sympathy. Of this book the Encyclopedia Britannica says:

The publication of Uncle Tom's Cabin, in book form in March. 1852, was a factor which must be reckoned in summing up the many causes of the Civil War. The book sprang into unexampled popularity and was translated into at least twenty-three languages. Mrs. Stowe then re-enforced her story with A Key to Uncle Tom's Cabin, in which she accumulated a large number of documents and testimonials against the Great Evil.

Other books were written to inflame the North on the subject of slavery. Among them was another written by Mrs. Stowe, Deed, A Tale of the Dismal Swamp, which doubtless met with great popularity. In 1857, a young man, Hinton Rowan Helper, was led to write a book, The Impending Crisis, in which he added "fuel to the flame." It is at once a curiosity in literature and one of the most diabolical books that was ever published. Accepting the Census figures he mentions that at the South there were 6,181,177 Whites, of whom 347,536 were slave owners. Allowing five persons to a family, there were about three times as many non-slaveholders as slaveholders.

Notwithstanding there were at the South about three non-slaveholders to every slaveholder, and every White man was a voter. Helper ascribes to slaveholders a virtual superiority. He declares page 44: "Never were the poorer classes of a people, and these classes so largely in the majority, and all inhabiting the same country, so basely duped, so adroitly swindled, or so damnably outraged." Then on page 96: "Except among the non-slaveholders, who besides being kept in the grossest ignorance, are under the restraints of iniquitous laws, patriotism has ceased to exist within her borders." But instead of there being any deplorable condition in North Carolina at that period it was rich in accomplishment, contentment, and happiness reigned. The public schools, begun in 1840, now had 177,000 White pupils, of whom 18,000 were in academies and at the University.

The exports of the United States for the year 1858 were: product of the North, $45,308,541; products of the North and South, $34,667,591; products of the South, $193,405,961. Total, $273,392,093.

The imports were $313,610,000. The products of the South were much more valuable than those of the North.

Confining ourselves to Helper's view, we see millions of White people at the South—with no sense. He makes some extracts and writes, "These extracts show conclusively that immediate and independent political action on the part of the non-slaveholding Whites of the South is with them not only a public duty, but also of the utmost importance. If not, they will be completely degraded to a social and political level with the Negroes," etc., etc.

Such was Helper's propaganda. But most persons held a different view—that as long as the Africans were held as a subject race, every White person stood on a higher platform. There was a

great gulf between the races. In law, every White man was equal. However, such was the view Helper presented, and so he sought to organize the no slaveholding Whites of the South to accomplish his purpose.

And on page 155, he says he proposed to erect a banner:

Inscribed on the banner which we herewith unfold are the mottoes:

1. Thorough organization on the part of the no slaveholding whites of the South.

2. Ineligibility of slaveholders—never another vote to the trafficker in human flesh.

3. No cooperation with slaveholders in politics—no fellowship with them in religion—no affiliation with them in society.

4. No patronage to slaveholding merchants—no guest shall use slave waiting hotels—no fees to slaveholding lawyers—no employment of slaveholding physicians—no audience to slaveholding parsons.

5. No recognition of pro-slavery men except as ruffians, outlaws, and criminals.

6. Abrupt discontinuance of subscriptions to proslavery newspapers.

Then addressing the slaveholders, he says: "But, Sirs, Knights of the bludgeon, Cavaliers of the bowie knives and pistols, and Lords of the lash." He says as to the use of the world "gentleman," page 116, "An appellation which we would no sooner think of applying to a proslavery slaveholder or any other pro-slavery man than we would think of applying it to a border ruffian, a thief, or a murderer." And on page 140, "We contend that slaveholders are more cruel than common murderers of men." On page 139, he says, "We mean precisely what our words express when we say we believe thieves are, as a general rule, less amenable to the moral law than slaveholders," and then he shows how much worse a slaveholder is than a thief—such as: "Thieves practice deceit on the wise, but slaveholders take advantage of the ignorant." "We contend, moreover, that slaveholders are more criminal than common murderers."

Such was the denunciation of the slaveholders—worse than thieves and murderers!

In an address to the non-slaveholders, he says:

Non-slaveholders of the South, farmers, mechanics, and workingmen, we take this occasion to assure you that the slaveholders, the arrogant demagogues whom you have elected to offices of honor and profit, have hoodwinked you, trifled with you, and used you as mere tools for the consummation of their wicked designs.

Indeed, it is our honest conviction that all the proslavery slaveholders deserve to be at once reduced to a parallel with the basest criminals that lie fettered within the cells of our public prisons. Were it possible for the whole number to be gathered together and transformed into four equal gangs of licensed robbers, ruffians, thieves, and murders, society would suffer less from their atrocities than it does now.

One of his appeals to the cupidity of the non-slave-holders is illustrative of his argument:

South of Mason and Dixon's line, we, the non-slave-holders, have 331,902,120 acres of land, the present market value of which is, as previously stated, only $5.34 per acre; by abolishing slavery, we expect to enhance the value to an average of at least $28.07 per acre, and thus realize an average net increase of more than seventy-five hundred million dollars.

Then on page 128, he addresses the slaveholders:

Henceforth, Sirs we are demandants, not supplicants.

It is for you to decide whether we are to have justice peaceably or by violence, for whatever consequences may follow, we are determined to have it one way or another..

Do you aspire to become the victims of white no slaveholders vengeance by day and of barbarous massacre by Negroes at night?

Would you be instrumental in bringing upon yourselves, your wives and your children, a fate too terrible to contemplate? Shall history cease to cite, as an instance of unexampled cruelty, the massacre of St. Bartholomew, because the World—the South—shall have furnished a more direful scene of atrocity and carnage?

We would not wantonly pluck a single hair from your heads—but we have endured long, we have endured much, slaves only of the most despicable class would endure more. And now, Sirs, you must emancipate them—or we will emancipate them for you.

And now, Sirs, we have thus laid down our ultimatum. What are you going to do about it? Something dreadful as a matter of course. Perhaps you will dissolve the Union again. Do it if you dare. Our motto, and we would have you to understand it, is the abolition of slavery, and the perpetuation of the American Union. If by any means you do succeed in your miserable attempts to take the South out of the Union today, we will bring her back tomorrow; if she goes away with you, she will return without you.

He proposed that "sometime during this year, next, or the year after, let there be a general convention of non-slave-holders from every State in the Union, to deliberate on the momentous issues no pending, First, let them adopt measures for holding in constraint the diabolical excesses of the oligarchy, and so on. If need be, let the delegates to this convention continue in session one or two weeks."

He then addresses the Northern people:

Freemen of the North! we earnestly entreat you to think of these things. Heretofore, as mere Free Soilers, you have approached but half way to the line of your duty; now for your sakes and for ours, and for the purpose of perpetuating this glorious Republic, which your Fathers and ours founded in a perennial avenue of blood, we ask you in all seriousness to organize yourselves as one man under the banner of Liberty, and to aid us in exterminating slavery, which is the only thing that militates against our complete aggrandizement as a Nation. In this extraordinary crisis of affairs, no man can be a true patriot without first becoming an Abolitionist.

This doctrine found willing hearts to agree to it. The Christian societies gladly accepted anything defamatory of the slaveholders and this publication was timely.

In Lincoln's great campaign for the Senatorship, he had declared that this government could not endure permanently half slave and half free. "It will become all one thing -or all the other."

While Lincoln's words were being echoed throughout the North, Helper's book was published. Its value as an aid to the movement against slavery was immediately seen by the Republican leaders, and, under the title of A Compendium of the Impending Crisis, and bearing the indorsement of sixty-four members of Congress and well-known Republicans, it was distributed throughout the North and West in batches of 100,000 copies, and put into the homes.

The potency of its effect in arraying the masses of the North against the Southern people cannot be estimated. There is no better illustration of its general effect on the Northern mind than the conduct of Rev. Mr. Worth, who brought a copy of it to North Carolina. On being asked why he did not abide by the North Carolina laws, he replied: "I have no respect for North Carolina laws, for they are enacted by adulterous drunkards and gamblers." He did not quote Helper's words, but he had his idea.

Helper's suggestion that the Negroes might arise in insurrection may have inflamed John Brown to make his attempt leading to that horrible episode, which, in its result—the conferring of sainthood on that despicable scoundrel—illustrates the feeling of the Northern fanatics and embittered the people of the South, non-slaveholders as well as slaveholders. The election for Congress was held after a bitter campaign. Helper's book played its part well. While only sixty-four Republican Congressmen distributed this book, they succeeded in almost doubling the number of Republican members elected.

And, when Congress met, the Republicans came near to having a majority. They nominated John Sherman, of Ohio, for Speaker. He was one of the sixty-four members of Congress who had signed a paper indorsing Helper's Impending Crisis, and was instrumental in distributing the book by batches of 100,000.

The Democrats introduced a resolution that no one who had indorsed Helper's book was fit to be a speaker (Howe, p. 386). A violent debate followed, and the excitement at times reached such a pitch that there was great danger of a riot on the floor of the House.

One Senator wrote: "So violent is the feeling that the members on both sides are mostly armed with deadly weapons, and it is said that the friends of each are armed in the galleries." Another Senator wrote: "I believe every man in both houses is armed with a revolver—some with two— and a bowie knife." Helper's words, dear to Republican hearts, were uttered in Congress. (Howe, p. 388). Lovejoy, among other intemperate expressions, said: "Slaveholding is worse than robbery, than piracy, than polygamy." That was the doctrine of the Democrats, and "the doctrine of devils as well," and that there was no place in the universe outside of the five limits of hell and the Democratic party where the practice and prevalence of such a doctrine would not be a disgrace. There followed a great uproar.

And Potter, a big Republican member from Wisconsin, was conspicuous in the melee, shouting and gesticulating like one beside himself. And for a time, Lovejoy and Potter became immensely

popular in the North (Howe, p. 388).

More than two months passed before the House could elect a speaker, and the feeling among the Congressmen and the lobbymen at Washington was shared by the people in their homes. Some months passed—and an Abolitionist was elected President. First South Carolina seceded, and then other Southern States. The President, Mr. Buchanan, held that the Constitution did not give Congress the right to make war on a State, and Congress, instead of declaring war, asked the Northern States to arrange for the seceded States to return.

Mr. Lincoln, becoming President, stated in his inaugural: "In your hands, and not in mine, is the momentous issue of Civil War. The Government will not assail you."

Then, presently, his cabinet having agreed to evacuate Fort Sumter, he let that be known as many rejoiced: but on April 1, he changed his mind. He would start a war. Why? How much did the spirit of The Impending Crisis, at work in the hearts of the Republicans in their homes, lead to Lincoln's change of heart? Had there been no such book, would Lincoln have precipitated the war against the Southern States?

Helper's book had done much in making the foundation on which that spirit was built. And again, was his vision of a Negro insurrection indulged in by his co-workers!

3. Nullification, North and South

The subject of Nullification is a particularly apt subject for our consideration at the present time. It is true that our conception of the meaning of Nullification has gradually changed during the last one hundred and sixty years—yet the subject is a much discussed one at the present date. Such subjects as "The High Cost of Nullification." "Ethics of Nullification," "Sanctity of the Law," etc., are familiar to everyone who reads the national periodicals.

What historical basis did the States of the Union have for their belief in Nullification? According to the peace treaty with Great Britain, signed in Paris in 1783, the independence of each State was recognized. And as a Sovereign State, each had the right to remain independent or to delegate such power as that State deemed wise in case of a union. And when the Constitution was adopted—after the obvious failure of the Union under the Articles of Confederation—some States held that a State had the right to nullify any and all laws not specifically delegated to the government by the several States. This theory of government was first embodied in the Virginia and Kentucky Resolutions of 1798. These resolutions from the pens of Madison and Jefferson, respectively, declared alien and sedition acts unconstitutional. They set forth the doctrine of States' Rights, according to which it was claimed, first, that when the Constitution was formed, the States by a common agreement united to create the national Government and entrusted to it certain powers; second, that the national Government so created was authorized to act simply as the agent of the States, which were the real sovereigns, and to do only those things which were specifically granted to it in the compact of the Constitution; and, third, that the right to decide whether the national Government did or did not act according to the terms of the compact belonged to the States alone, the creators of the national Government.

The legislature of Kentucky went a step farther the following year and added to these premises the logical conclusion that if a State should decide that the national government had acted contrary to the agreement—for example, by passing unconstitutional laws in Congress—the State should declare those laws null and void. How it worked out in actual practice was not made clear at the time. Its enemies declared that it would not work at all. They pointed out how it might easily happen that some States would choose to nullify one law, other States another law, until the national government became an object of ridicule and its laws reduced to confusion. These were the arguments of Washington and Adams, who favored, as the final judge for all the States in matters concerning the interpretation of the Constitution, the Supreme Court of the United Stales, on the ground that in this way only could the dignity of the national government be safeguarded and the uniformity of the national laws throughout the Union be secured.

The principles of the Virginia and Kentucky Resolutions led to many conflicts between States and the National government, particularly in New England during the War of 1812, when that

section was opposed to the policy of the National Government, and reached its height when it played an important part in bringing on the War Between the States -between the North and South in 1861.

On July 4, 1854, at Framingham, Mass., a great concourse of people gave expression to their rebellion. They first burnt a copy of the Act of Congress, called "The Fugitive Slave Law;" next the decision of Judge Loring in the case of Bevas; next the charge of Judge Curtis to the Federal Grand Jury; and, lastly, burnt the Constitution as "The Covenant of Death and Agreement with Hell"—"at which, from that vast crowd, a tremendous shout of 'Amen,' went up to heaven in ratification of the deed"—and Garrison, the leader, declared that "the Free States should withdraw from the Union—and have no Union with slaveholders"—and it is said that he and some of his followers would no longer vote as citizens.

In New York, the great leader, Seward, announced the doctrine. "A Higher Law" than the Constitution, and declared "An Irrepressible Conflict," and this new doctrine was received with enthusiasm. The Constitution was not to be obeyed. There was a Higher Law; and so the rebellion spread. There was a clash between the Constitution and the "Law of God," said the rebels— and they assumed the role of Ambassadors of the Deity. Vermont and Massachusetts were the first States to act—then followed Pennsylvania and other States. The action in Wisconsin was most vigorous. There, as stated by Daniel Wait Howe, President of the Indiana Historical Society, in his Political History of Secession, the Governor, the Supreme Court, the Legislature and the people of Wisconsin "nullified the Act of Congress;" and that State became the companion of twelve other Northern States in the rebellion.

Books were written to inflame the Northern people against the Southern people who stood for the Constitution. At length, in 1858, John Brown, crazed with the subject, after various murderous episodes, attempted to start an insurrection of the slaves in Virginia. His attempt failed and he suffered the penalty. While the people of the South regarded him as a monster— like those who led the Negroes of Hayti to massacre there, eminent leaders at the North—such as Emerson, Theodore Parker, and Wendell Phillips—eulogized Brown as "a New Saint, making the gallows as glorious as the Cross," saying "the Almighty would welcome him home in Heaven," and that "John Brown has gone to Heaven." So that murderer and felon became the incarnation of the noblest sentiment of many citizens of the Northern States, and worship of him crystallized their religious sentiment.

However, at the South, the relations between the African slaves and the White families with whom they had been raised were such that whatever efforts were made to stir up insurrections were fruitless. But the indignation of the Whites of the South at

Northern malevolence was boundless, the hero of the Northern Abolitionists appearing to them to be devil incarnate. Then other unfriendly actions at the North likewise contributed fuel to the flame. So when Congress met in December, 1859, there was turmoil.

Says Howe:

The account of the scenes in Congress then would be incredible were they not vouched for by reliable authority. "One day a member from New York was speaking, and a pistol accidentally fell from his pocket. Some members became wild with passion. A scene of pandemonium ensued

-and a bloody contest was imminent." A United States Senator wrote: "The members on both sides are mostly armed with deadly weapons, and it is said that the friends of each are armed in the galleries." And another Senator wrote: "I believe every man in both Houses is armed with a revolver—some with two—and a bowie knife besides!"

The feeling among the members of Congress was shared by the people both North and South in their homes. And "generally throughout the North, more especially in New England, the voice of the clergy thundered from every pulpit in denunciation of slavery and the slaveholders of the South." The higher law made slavery a sin.

Many additions were made to the ranks of the Abolitionists, and especially among the German inhabitants of the Western States. Besides the descendants of the early German settlers, in the recent decades more than a million other Germans had settled in the West, and this element was stirred by many new political refugees, who readily embraced Seward's doctrine of "The Higher Law," as they knew nothing of the history of our country and cared nothing for our Constitution. "We are the Ambassadors of the Creator to establish His Higher Law" was their sentiment.

The bitter antagonism developed by this rebellion against the Constitution and denunciation of the slaveholders reached its height during the political campaign of 1860, and while the candidate for President supported by "The Higher Law Party" received only 1,860,452 votes out of a total of 4,680,700, he was elected by receiving 180 electoral votes, all in the Northern States, the other candidates receiving only 84, chiefly at the South. Howe gives a careful account of the voting in the Northern States.

The slaveholders of the seven cotton States, considering the condition—possible insurrection and other trouble -thought it best to withdraw from the Union in peace. The cause of their withdrawal was certainly the attitude of the "Higher Law" people towards the Constitution.

As for the right of a State to withdraw, that was thought to be beyond question. The States had been declared sovereign States by Great Britain and as such had agreed to the Articles of Confederation, which were to be perpetual, but, after six years, eleven States, being sovereign States, withdrew from it. And in so doing, Virginia and New York declared the right of any State to withdraw from the new Union.

Washington, as a delegate from Virginia, presided over the Convention that framed the new Constitution, and certainly assented this declaration by Virginia. The Continental Congress accepted ratification and declaration on the part of these two States; and ten years later, when Rhode Island applied for admission to the new Union, she likewise declared the right of a State to withdraw from it just as all the States had withdrawn from the perpetual Union 1781. There was no objection then made to those declarations, which were a part of the ratifications of the Constitution. So the right to withdraw was recognized. And the Supreme Court of the United States, in its opinion filed December 22, 1862 (Vol. LXVII), said under our Constitution neither the President nor Congress had right to make war on a State; and the Court apparently knew of nothing to prevent a State from lawfully seceding. It said: "The war between the Northern and Southern States was to settle that claim by 'wager of battle.'"

4. The States Made the Union

In the October Veteran, I called attention to President Lincoln's disregard of historical facts when they stood in the way of his desire. It struck his fancy to assert that the Union made the States and not the States made the Union. It suited his purpose to declare that, and doubtless he considered that it would be an appealing idea and reach the hearts of the Northern people, for he was gifted with a certain sort of wisdom.

In his address at Gettysburg, a year after that memorable battle, he made a similar venture into the realms of fancy, doubtless being animated by the same sort of wisdom, closing his address with this appealing sentence: "We here highly resolve that these dead shall not have died in vain; that this nation, under God, shall have a new birth of freedom, and that government of the people, by the people, and for the people shall not perish from the earth."

It has been said that this address received but little attention throughout the Northern States at the time, but in later years, when the North found it interesting to magnify Mr. Lincoln, it has been regarded as of surpassing excellence.

The basis of all fine portrayal is accuracy of statement. The delineation should not be foreign to the subject. Mr. Lincoln paid slight attention to this rule when seeking to enlist the patriotic people of the North in his propaganda for a consolidated nation. It is apparent that this appealing thought—that "government by the people" "shall not perish"—is entirely at variance with the fundamentals of the tremendous conflict he was waging.

The system of government established by the Constitution in 1788 between eleven States was not affected by the accession of two more States after its establishment. Neither was the system affected by the withdrawal of seven States in 1860-61. It remained perfect as to the twenty-nine States that remained in the Union. Indeed, instead of the system perishing by the withdrawal of some of the States—since those States continued under the same system under virtually the same Constitution—the effect, instead of destroying the system, was to duplicate it, and thus give the people of the world another example of that form of government whose excellence had awakened general admiration.

Moreover, President Lincoln's characterization as a nation, of the system under the Constitution he had sworn to observe and maintain, is erroneous. Though Jefferson did not write the Constitution, there was not a man concerned in writing it who had the purpose to create a nation in the legal meaning of that word. Indeed, although, when proposing to invest certain high powers in the government, they had freely used the word "national" in the rough draft, when the Constitution was prepared for adoption, the word "nation" was entirely eliminated. The purpose

was not to create a nation, but just as Jefferson and everybody else desired, to continue the Confederation, making it a more perfect one, as the Constitution says, "between the States." A nation is responsive to the popular will; a majority of the people rule. In 1860, Mr. Lincoln was elected, but failed to get majority of votes at the polls. His election was a striking denial of the idea that our government is that of a nation. So, likewise at the recent presidential election, although one candidate received more than seventeen million votes, being two million majority over his opponent a change of only about 275,000 votes would have elected the defeated candidate in spite of the two million popular majority against him.

Our system is a Confederation of States, set up by the colonies after having freed themselves from a monarchy. Democracy is the fundamental basis of our state governments. We have forty-eight democracies. Regarding each State as a sovereignty, we present the world an example of forty-eight sovereign democracies, each free from the control or interference of any other, but all subject to the joint control of the forty-eight in certain specified matters. This secures to each State the greatest freedom.

The separate entity of the several sovereign States is recognized in the Constitution from first to last. The Constitution was to go into effect "between any nine States adopting it," not over them.

As a sovereign State might in itself establish an aristocracy, or limited monarchy, such as Hamilton and John Adams are said to have favored, to prevent that, the ratifying States agreed to guarantee each other that no such fate should befall any. Now, suppose there had been no such guarantee, and that Massachusetts and New York had been persuaded to have a limited monarchy. Again, any State was liable to be invaded and conquered. So, the ratifying States agreed to protect every State against invasion. Certainly, that would have been unnecessary had the States been consolidated into a single nation. Yet it is to be remembered that in 1814, Great Britain hoped and expected to acquire Massachusetts and other States bordering Canada, and perhaps had not the war then ended she might have done so. Indeed, when considering the new Constitution which for two years she rejected, Rhode Island threatened to connect hers with some European country. The Constitution throughout bears evidence that our Union is a federation of States, each State retaining every power and right of a sovereign State, not specified as delegated to the Union.

Now, what is the relation of the States to the government? Consider legislation by Congress. Legislation is by the States represented in the House according to their own importance, while in the Senate there is equality; but, for expediency's sake, there are two members, instead of a single member, to represent the State.

Thus, there can be no legislation except by the assent of a majority of the States; and it is expressly agreed that no State shall be deprived of her equal representation in the Senate without her consent.

Then consider the election of the Executive. Were this a nation, the President would be elected by a majority of the people; but it is not so. The States elect the President. Ordinarily, in this election, they have votes according to their importance. The legislature of each State is to appoint or provide for the appointment of a number of electors equal to its representation in Congress, and these Electors, acting for their States, select the President. In event they fail, then the State

delegation in the House of Representatives act as Electors, and, in the name of their State, give a single vote to some candidate. It requires a majority of the States to elect. So, in 1801, Jefferson, who received ten votes of sixteen, was elected; and, in 1825, John Quincy Adams got thirteen votes out of twenty-four and was elected. No matter how small or how great, each State has a single vote.

So, we see that the government, legislative and executive, is by the States. Certainly, the people of each State constitute that State. The sovereignty of the State resides in the people, and the Union is a confederation of forty-eight sovereignties. The Union is governed by the States. This government has been declared to be the achievement of the highest wisdom known to the human race. There have been doubtless a hundred conquerors who have created a hundred nations, and there have been some famous confederations in Europe, but our American system of a confederation of sovereign States, in a Union, under a constitution, stands as a beacon light directing the people of the world into the path leading to pure democracy, and the greatest personal freedom, the greatest happiness and prosperity. It is the acme of wisdom in government. This system was not disturbed by the withdrawal of seven States from the Union, and, although President Lincoln had sworn to support it, he announced a doctrine, not founded on any provision of the Constitution, that the Constitution created a nation; then he solemnly declared that by conquering the Southern States, bringing their unwilling people again into the Union was to give a new birth to freedom! While at the time the Northern people did not make much of that sentiment, of late it is greatly admired.

Certainly, a return of the States without a war was greatly to be desired; and steps had been taken to that end -and Mr. Lincoln personally may have been willing—but he was led to change and to seek to enforce his will by arms.

Some persons erroneously suppose that Mr. Lincoln began the war with the purpose of abolishing slavery, freeing the Negro slaves at the South. So England, when she established Colonies, forbade them to manufacture anything and required them to trade only with Great Britain. 'To increase their products," she supplied them with African slaves and sold them her convicts. The war of 1775 was for economic purposes. So the war of 1861 was for economic purposes. Mr. Lincoln was urged on by the Northwestern folks who did not wish to lose the trade of the Mississippi River, and by the financial and commercial people of the Northeast, who could point to the ten per cent tariff of the Southern Confederacy and to the cotton exports, which, in 1859, had been $161,434,923 out of a total of $278,302,080; while the South furnished perhaps the greater part of the residue!

So it came about that on March 30, 1861, the New York Times, speaking ex cathedra, said: "It is no longer an abstract question, one of a constitutional construction, or reserved or delegated powers of the States to the Federal Government, but of material existence, and moral position both at home and abroad." The North had to have the South even by conquest! And so Mr. Lincoln started the war. He had no purpose to interfere with slavery, but held that under the Constitution, neither he nor Congress could interfere with slavery. After four years of war, he said, in his second Inaugural: "Neither party expected for the war the magnitude or the duration it has already attained. Each looked for an easier triumph." Yes, he certainly looked for an easier triumph. We may well believe that had he fully realized what was to come, he would have listened to the pleadings of W. H. Seward, his Secretary of State, and have sought a peaceful

restoration of the Union. Instead, he took his own course. And, after declining, in February, 1865, at Hampton Roads, to consider anything but unconditional surrender, in his Inaugural of March 4, he declared: "Yet, if God wills that it continue until all the wealth piled by the bondsman's two hundred and fifty years of unrequited toil shall be sunk, and every drop of blood drawn with the lash shall be paid by another drawn with the sword, as was said three thousand years ago, still it must be said, the judgments of the Lord are true and righteous altogether." And it was all his own doing—from start to finish. So he conquered the South for economic reasons, as most of the wars have been waged in Europe. And it brought him the fame of unnecessarily causing the deaths of more human beings and of destroying more wealth and property, and of causing more sorrow, distress, and sectional hatred than attaches to the name of any other person that ever lived up to that time. And yet there are those who speak of him as a good, kindly man!

5. Nullification, North and South

Some time back there was an interesting incident in the United States Senate. Senator Walsh, of Montana—very naturally for him and very innocent of treading on anybody's toes—said that all the members of Congress who had served in the Confederate armies had been, "technically," "traitors and rebels." Whereupon Senator Blease of South Carolina, jumped on him with both feet and declared that if anyone had said that outside of the chamber, the "Old Harry" would have been to pay. In the following I have taken occasion to write on the subject historically, examining Mr. Lincoln's premise that the Union began in 1774, and that no State could get out of that Union then created, and then, passing on to the Union under the Constitution of 1789.

Our daily life of contentment and happiness has a tendency to obliterate the grounds on which the South thought the States had a right to withdraw from the Union. It is the mere right that I wish to talk about.

The colonies, having joined in a Declaration of Independence, continued to cooperate, expecting to enter into a Confederacy. A plan of confederation was framed, but it was not agreed to until May, 1781.

The second article of this Confederation is: "Each State retains its sovereignty, freedom, and independence, and every power, jurisdiction, and right which is not expressly delegated to the United States in Congress assembled."

Third: "The said States hereby severally enter into a firm league of friendship with each other."

Thirteenth: "And the articles of this confederation shall be inviolately observed by every State and the Union be perpetual; nor shall any alteration at any time hereafter be made in any of them unless such alteration is agreed to in a Congress of the

United States and afterwards confirmed by the legislature of every State."

After that, by treaty of peace with Great Britain, it was declared by the king of Great Britain that each State—naming each of them—was "a free, sovereign, and independent State."

That Confederation existed until 1787, when Virginia proposed to supplant it with a new one. This new one was to go into effect between any nine States that might ratify it. When the new Constitution was submitted to the States, eleven of them ratified it, and it went into operation between them in 1788. Under it a President was to be elected in February, 1789, by electors chosen in January, 1789. Somehow, New York did not vote in that election; North Carolina and Rhode Island did riot, for they had not ratified the Constitution; so, when Washington was

elected President in February, 1789, only ten States voted. Certainly, North Carolina and Rhode Island were no longer united to the other States. As to them, the Confederacy that was to be perpetual had been broken up by the other eleven States, and they were left alone.

When Virginia and New York ratified they said that "the States reserved the right to resume the powers delegated to the United States;" so likewise did Rhode Island.

And that was the general understanding. Their ratification with that declaration in it was not objected to by anyone. The right to resume the powers delegated to the Congress was exercised by the States when they broke up the Confederation; and when North Carolina and Rhode Island were out of the new Union, they had full sovereign powers.

Although the first Confederation was to be perpetual and not subject to change except by unanimous consent. the States, by reason of their sovereign power, could withdraw from it—and did so.

Later, when a new Union was made between the States, they retained the same sovereign powers, and some so declared in adopting the new agreement, without objection; and they omitted to say that the new Union was to be perpetual; and having also omitted to say that the States retained all the powers not delegated, they at once put that in the Constitution.

When the uninformed intelligence of the North ascribes to ministers of the gospel at the South, to our patriots who have been examples of high virtue and nobility of character, to the gentle ladies of the South the spirit of "traitors," and cite Aaron Burr and John Brown on one hand, and George Washington and Benjamin Franklin on the other the latter having said, "We must all hang together, or we will all hang separately," I remind them that when Washington raised his flag or January 2, 1776, at Boston—the very flag he had directed Betsy Ross to make—that flag bore the ensign of Great Britain along with the colors of the Washington coat-of-arms. It was as a subject of the king that he was claiming his rights as a British subject. The citizens of the seceded States were never subjects of any State but that of which they were citizens. They owed obedience and allegiance to their States and never to any other State. Whatever obedience they owed to the government of the United States was by virtue of the delegated authority of these several States which had now been withdrawn and had ended.

6. Ratification of the Constitution by Virginia, New York, and Rhode Island

Proceedings in the convention of Virginia, Wednesday, 25 June, 1788. Debates of the Convention.

On motion, ordered: That a committee be appointed to prepare and report a form of ratification, pursuant to the first resolution; and that his Excellency Governor Randolph, Mr. Nicholas, Mr. Madison, Mr. Marshall, and Mr. Corbin, compose the said committee.

His Excellency Governor Randolph reported, from the Committee appointed according to order, a form of ratification, which was read and agreed to by the convention, in the words following:

We, the delegates of the people of Virginia, duly elected in pursuance of a recommendation from the general assembly, and now met in convention, having fully and freely investigated and discussed the proceedings of the Federal Convention, and being prepared as well as the most mature deliberation hath enabled us to decide thereon. Do, in the name and in behalf of the people of Virginia, declare and make known that the powers granted under the Constitution being derived from the people of the United States may be resumed by them whensoever the same shall be perverted to their injury or oppression, and that every power not granted thereby remains with them and at their will: That, therefore, no right of any denomination can be cancelled, abridged, restrained, or modified by the Congress, by the Senate, or House of Representatives, acting in any capacity, by the President or any department or officer of the United States, except in the instances in which power is given by the Constitution for those purposes; and that, among other essential rights, the liberty of conscience and of the press cannot be cancelled, abridged, restrained, or modified by any authority of the United States.

With these impressions, with a solemn appeal to the searcher of hearts for the purity of our intentions and under the conviction, that, whatsoever imperfections may exist in the Constitution, ought rather to be examined in the mode prescribed therein than to bring the Union into danger by a delay, with a hope of obtaining amendments previous to the ratification:

We, the said Delegates, in the name and in behalf of the people of Virginia, do, by these presents, assent to and ratify the Constitution recommended on the 17th day of September, one thousand, seven hundred and eighty-seven, by the Federal Convention, for the government of the United States; hereby announcing to all those whom it may concern that the said Constitution is binding upon the said people, according to an authentic copy hereto annexed, in the words following:

On motion, Ordered, That the secretary of this convention cause to be engrossed, forthwith, two fair copies of the form of ratification and of the proposed Constitution of government, as recommended by the Federal Convention on the 17th day of September, one thousand seven hundred and eighty-seven.

And then the Convention adjourned until tomorrow morning twelve o'clock.

Motion of Thursday, the 26th of June, 1788

An engrossed form of the ratification agreed to yesterday containing the proposed constitution of government, as recommended by the Federal Convention on the seventeenth day of September, one thousand seven hundred and eighty-seven, being prepared by the secretary, was read and signed by the president in behalf of the convention.

On motion, Ordered, That the said ratification be transmitted by the president, in the name of this convention, to the United States in Congress assembled.

Ratification by New York and Rhode Island The ratification by New York, July 26, 1788:

We. the delegates of the people of New York... do declare and make known that the powers of government may be reassumed by the people whenever it shall become necessary to their happiness; that every power, jurisdiction, and right which is not by the said Constitution clearly delegated to the Congress of the United States, or the department of the government thereof, remains to the people of the several States, or to their respective State governments, to whom they may have granted the same.

We, the delegates of the people of Rhode Island and Plantations, duly elected, etc., do declare and make known....... That the powers of government may be resumed by the people whenever it shall become necessary to their happiness, etc. [as in the ratification of New York.]

7. Secession, Insurrection of the Negroes, and Northern Incendiarism

Secession was a right claimed by Virginia, New York and Rhode Island in their ratification of the Constitution and not denied by any but assented to by all.

Seven States seceded in the winter of 1860-61, and, on March 11, 1861, formed a new Confederacy of sovereign States with virtually the same Constitution as the United States. It created "a government proper," and the laws of Congress acted directly on individuals. The other Southern States seceded later when called on to engage in a war against this new Confederacy. Why was that first secession? African slavery had existed in every colony and State, and was particularly recognized and cared for in the Constitution, every State agreeing to return to the owner any fugitive slave. Without this recognition there could have been no Union. An eminent justice of the United States Supreme Court, Henry Baldwin, of Pennsylvania, had declared slavery "the cornerstone" of the Government (Johnson vs. Tompkins, 1 Baldwin). In time, the Northern States, whose shipping had brought many of the Negroes into this country, abandoned slavery. Still every man who held office swore to support the Constitution. There was only one honest way out of the obligation to respect slavery, and that was to withdraw from the Union.

Instead of doing this, the Northern States became the place for numerous combinations of persons formed to bring about and promote Negro revolt and insurrection in the South. No laws were passed by the Northern States to restrain them.

These persons encouraged Nat Turner's insurrection in Virginia in 1828, and a similar attempt was made near Wilmington, in North Carolina.

Thus it came about that a joint committee of the two Houses of the Legislature in North Carolina, in 1831, reported they were satisfied "that an extensive combination now exists to excite in the minds of the slaves and colored persons of this and the other slave States the feelings and opinions leading to insurrections." They also reported "the actual detection of the circulation of the incendiary publications and discovery of the designs," etc., "and we are led to fear the most ruinous consequences."

After that year the Abolition sentiment continued to grow at the North until, at length, a dozen Northern States nullified the Constitution and Acts of Congress, and, in Massachusetts, some persons even burned them! It was declared that those States "have permitted the open establishment of societies whose avowed object is to disturb the peace of other States." "They have incited by emissaries, books, and pictures the Negroes to servile insurrection." Although

Congress had no authority over Negro slavery, its table was covered with petitions for its abolition expressed in the harshest possible terms about the Southern people.

Every means was resorted to disturb the peace of the South. Besides the effort to promote insurrection, a fight was made against the article in the Constitution allowing the South representation for three-fifths of its slaves. A provision to that effect appeared in the Resolutions of the Hartford Convention, and it kept appearing year after year, although the motion to allow such representation had originally come from a Northern man. Then the provision in the Constitution for returning fugitive slaves was nullified.

Societies were formed to run off Negroes from the plantations by secret means, called "the Underground Railway." Hundreds were carried off. Nothing was done to prevent it.

None of these schemes was sufficient to solidify the people of the North till the idea of stopping "the extension of slavery" seized upon the politicians there. This was first tried in connection with the admission of the State of Missouri in 1820.

Out of the struggle which arose in 1820 came a Compromise act, which permitted Missouri to come in as a slave State but divided the rest of the outstanding territory by the parallel of 36° 30' North latitude. Under it the North got nine-tenths of the area.

There was no real probability of another slave State. But while the South was ready to yield to the dictates of nature, they were not so readily disposed to yield up their rights under the Constitution at the dictation of Northern fanatics. They claimed that the Constitution made no difference between slaves and other property, and that the country during its first 40 years acknowledged it in all its dealings. Witness the Treaty of Peace in 1814, when Great Britain agreed to pay for the slaves carried off, and did so. And even as late as 1856, Great Britain paid for the slaves that escaped from the Creole in 1841.

Out of this agitation sprang certain societies in the North who organized emigration to Kansas. Civil war ensued, and many were killed.

Then arose the Republican party, composed of many lawless elements, the Abolitionists, who burnt the Constitution, the Know-nothings, who burnt the Catholic churches, and the agitators who promoted rebellion in Kansas with Sharp's rifles.

Thence across the phantasm called "the Slave Power." In combination with the Abolitionists and the antislavery advocates everywhere, the writers and speakers of the North, foaming at the mouth with frenzy, tore to tatters the good name and fame of the Southern people and deluged the land with lectures and tracts upon the threatening approach of this terrible monster, "the Slave Power."

This excitement, which assumed a form of madness, was not abated when the Supreme Court of the United States in the Dred Scott case decided in 1857 that the Constitutional right was all on the side of the South. The Supreme Court was abused, as if the members were pirates and horse thieves. But it is a singular fact that six years after the war the same court decided there was no difference by the common law and the law of nations between slaves and other property. (Osborne vs. Nicholson, 13 Wallace, 661).

Then a defamatory book by that renegade Southerner named Helper had different treatment, and at the election in 1858 it was endorsed by the Republican Congressmen and widely circulated throughout the North. Its effect was notable. That party increased its membership in Congress from sixty-seven to nearly double that number. In it the author said to the slaveholders:

Henceforth, Sirs, we are demandants—not supplicants. It is for you to decide whether we are to have justice peaceably or by violence, for whatever consequence—we are determined to have it one way or another. Would you be instrumental in bringing upon yourselves, your wives and your children a fate too horrible to contemplate? Shall history cease to cite as an instance of unexampled cruelty the massacre of St. Bartholomew because the World—the South—shall have furnished a more direful scene of atrocity and carnage?

Such was the picture of slaughter proposed by the fanatic Abolitionists, and endorsed by the Republicans.

Then John Brown, who had committed many murders in Kansas, after raising a considerable sum of money in Boston and elsewhere and obtaining a supply of arms, on Sunday, October 16, 1859, started on his mission. With a force of seventeen Whites and five Negroes, he captured the arsenal at Harper's Ferry, expecting the slaves to rise. Brown was a rebel against both Virginia and the United States, for while he killed several citizens of Virginia, he attacked United States property and killed a United States marine. Brown was tried and executed. Then throughout the North, John Brown was said to have gone straight to Heaven—a saint! a "Lord High Admiral of the Almighty!"

When Congress met on the fifth day of December, 1859, the Republicans proposed John Sherman for Speaker. Thereupon, some Democrats offered a resolution that no man who endorsed Helper's Impending Crisis was fit to be Speaker. That raised such a conflict that a riot ensued, the members carrying pistols; and it was not until February 22 that the House organized by electing as Speaker an Old Line Whig. The House would not approve Negro insurrection after a conflict lasting more than two months.

In 1860 a man named Willis was arrested at Greenville, South Carolina, for distributing insurrectionary literature to the Negroes.

Then came the election of President. The Republicans met at Chicago May 16, 1860, and nominated Abraham Lincoln as President.

On the question at issue Lincoln was as unbending as the most radical of his party. He had voted for the Wilmot Proviso in 1846. Later Lincoln subscribed $100 to promote John Brown's lawless proceedings (Herndon and Weik, Life of Lincoln, Vol. II, page 380). Lincoln and the other Republicans pretended to condemn John Brown, but when Stephen A. Douglas introduced a resolution to punish those people who seek to incite slave insurrections, "Abraham Lincoln in his speech at New York, declared it was a seditious speech"—"his press and party hooted it." "It received their jeers and jibes." (See Stephens' Pictorial History, and Nicolay and Hay, Complete Works of Abraham Lincoln, Vol. I, p. 611).

Lincoln was elected by a minority vote and was soon called upon to meet the issue of secession. The people of the South had realized the possible results. With the people and the State

governments of the North making a saint out of a man who had planned and started to murder the slaveholders—the Whites of the South—and the Northern States all going in favor of that party which sympathized with and protected those engaged in such plans, naturally there were in every Southern State, those who thought it best to guard against such massacres by separating from those States where John Brown was deified.

When the news came that Lincoln was elected, the South Carolina Legislature, being in session, called a State Convention. When the Convention met, it withdrew from the Union. In its declaration it said: "Those States have encouraged and assisted thousands of our slaves to leave their homes; and those who remain have been incited by emissaries, books and pictures to servile insurrection. For twenty-five years this agitation has been steadily increasing, until it has now secured to its aid the power of the common government." So, South Carolina met the threat of massacre, and took final action against the Chicago platform, which flaunted the decision of the Supreme Court. Had Lincoln professed obedience to the Court, he would have been accepted as President, and South Carolina trusting in the Court for protection against massacre would not have seceded.

Now why did South Carolina lead the Cotton States into withdrawing from the Union? What was the cause?

We find it stated by President James Buchanan. In his annual message to Congress December 19, 1859, he said (Richardson, Vol. V, page 554):

It ought never to be forgotten that however great may have been the political advantages resulting from the Union, these would all prove to be as nothing, should the time ever arrive when they cannot be enjoyed without serious danger to the personal safety of the people of fifteen members of the Confederacy.

If the peace of the domestic fireside throughout these States should ever be invaded, if the mothers of families within this extensive region should not be able to retire to rest at night without suffering dreadful apprehensions of what may be their own fate and that of their children before the morning, it would be in vain to account to such a people the political benefits which result to them from the Union.

Self-preservation is the first law of nature, and therefore any state of society in which the sword is all the time suspended over the heads of the people must at last become intolerable.

In his message of December 3, 1860, President Buchanan said to Congress, and virtually to the people of the North (Richardson, Vol. V, p. 626):

The long continued and intemperate interference of the Northern people with the question of slavery in the Southern States has at length produced its natural effects.

I have long foreseen and often forewarned my countrymen of the new impending danger. The immediate peril arises not so much from these causes as from the fact that the incessant and violent agitation of the slavery question throughout the North for the last quarter of a century has at length produced its malign influence on the slaves and inspired them with vague notions of freedom. Hence a sense of security no longer exists around the family altar. This feeling of peace

at home has given place to apprehensions of servile insurrections.

Many a matron throughout the South retires at night in dread of what may befall herself and children before the morning.

Self-preservation is the first law of nature: and has been implanted in the heart of man by his Creator for the wisest purpose. But let us take warning in time and remove the cause of danger.

It cannot be denied that for five and twenty years the agitation of the North against slavery had been incessant. In 1835 pictorial hand-bills and inflammatory appeals were circulated extensively throughout the South of a character to excite the passions of the slaves and, in the language of General Jackson, to stimulate them to insurrection and produce all the horrors of a servile war.

At the Presidential election in 1860 the Republican Party was greatly agitated over the Helper book which instigated massacre. Lincoln and Seward would not say that they were for massacre, but the Abolitionists had the vision of the X-ray and could see through such false pretenses.

The doctrine of both—"the irrepressible conflict" of Seward and "a house divided against itself cannot stand" of Lincoln—pointed directly to bloodshed. The Abolitionists voted for Lincoln, and Wendell Phillips, who rejoiced at his election, said in a speech at Tremont Temple, Boston, a few days later:

There was a great noise at Chicago, much pulling of wires and creaking of wheels, then forth stept Abraham Lincoln. But John Brown was behind the curtain, and the cannon of March 4 will only echo the rifles at Harpers Ferry * * * The Republican party have undertaken the problem the solution of which will force them to our position. Not Mr. Seward's "Union and Liberty" which he stole from Webster's "Liberty first" (a long pause) then "Union afterwards" (Phillips, Speeches and Lectures, pp. 294, 314).

South Carolina, having the largest Negro population in the Union, thought to seek safety by withdrawal from the Union. And sure enough Lincoln made the Negro—not Union—his first thought, and he would not agree to any compromise, would not come to Washington, at the request of President Buchanan, to help him preserve the peace, and finally, urged on by the tariff interests, sent troops to Fort Pickens and Fort Sumter, and brought on the war. At the last of August, 1862, Pope, who was in command of the army near Washington, was defeated, and, in September, President Lincoln thought that by threatening to free the Negroes at the South he might help his prospects in the War. Delegations from the churches in Chicago also addressed him. The radicals in Congress threatened to refuse appropriations. (Welling in Rice, Reminiscences, p. 533). He said he hesitated. It was to be a war measure. There were those who deemed it a barbarity to start an insurrection of the Negroes. As to that, President Lincoln said:

"Nor do I urge objections of a moral nature in view of possible consequences of insurrection and massacre at the South."

The French newspaper at New York said: "Does the Government at Washington mean to say that, on January 1st, it will call for a servile war to aid in the conquest of the South? And after the Negroes have killed the Whites, the Negroes themselves must be drowned in their own blood." Many other persons in America and England asked the same question, but Lincoln contented himself with what he said. Governor Morton of Indiana was for the insurrection. Charles Sumner, in his speech, at Faneuil Hall said of the Southern slaveholders: "When they rose against a paternal government they set an example of insurrection. They cannot complain if their slaves, with better reason, follow it." And a few months after Lincoln's proclamation Wendell Phillips said in a speech which was much applauded: "I am for conciliation but not for conciliating the slaveholders. Death to the system, and death or exile to the master is the only motto. Confiscate their lands, colonize them, sell them, with the guaranty of the government to the loyal Massachusetts man or New Yorker." And so talked Winter Davis, Ben Wade and Thaddeus Stevens.

Lincoln's proclamation had no peaceful humanitarian purpose, for he excepted the part of the country under his authority and applied it to a part of the country where he had none at the time. In that part he incited the Negroes to insurrection, and had no power to control them. This made his action very criminal.

It is difficult for us now after 72 years to realize the amount of hatred the Southerners had to bear. The Northern papers at the beginning of the war counselled the most demoniac treatment. One paper, the New York Courier and Enquirer, advised that "the Negroes be let loose on the Whites, men, women and children indiscriminately, and to prostrate the levees on the Mississippi so as to drown the rebels on the lower Mississippi just as we would drown out rats infesting the hull of a ship." Welles, Lincoln's Secretary of the Navy, states in his Diary (Vol. II, pp. 277, 278) that the North counted on insurrection of the Negroes to keep the Southerners engaged. There is no doubt that Lincoln shared in the same expectations as a result of his emancipation proclamation. In a letter to Vice-President Hannibal Hamlin, six days later he said: "The time of its effect Southward has not come; but Northward the effect should be instantaneous." The most obvious form of the "effect Southward" would of course have been an insurrection and massacre, but none occurred because of the humanity with which the slaves had been treated.

At length in May, 1863, it was arranged that there should be a general insurrection throughout the South, and it is not at all likely that Lincoln was ignorant of so widespread and all important an affair. In Official Records of the Rebellion, Series I, Vol. LI, Part 11, Supplemental p. 736, is found the following—preserved and printed by the Government:

War Department, C.S. A.,

Richmond, Va., July 18,1863.

His Excellency T.O. Moore,

Governor of Louisiana,

Shreveport, La.

Sir: I have the honor to enclose a letter from A.S. Montgomery, found in the mail of a federal steamer, plying between New Bern and Norfolk, which was captured by our troops. You will perceive that it discloses a plan for a general insurrection of the slaves in the Confederacy on 1st of August next..

James A. Seddon, Secretary of War.

Confidential.

Washington, D.C., May 19, 1863.

General: A plan has been formed for a simultaneous movement to sever the rebel communications throughout the whole South, which has been sent to some general in each military department in the seceded States, in order that they may act in concert and thus secure success.

The plan is to induce the Blacks to make a simultaneous movement of rising, on the night of the 1st of August next, over the entire States in rebellion, to arm themselves with any and every kind of weapons that may come to hand, and commence operations by burning all the railroad and country bridges, and tear up railroad tracks, and to destroy telegraph lines, etc., and then take to the woods, swamps, or the mountains, where they may emerge as occasion may offer for provisions and for further depredations. No blood is to be shed except in self-defense. The corn will be ripe about the 1st of August and with this and hogs running wild in the woods, and by foraging upon the plantations by night, they can subsist. This is the plan in substance, and if we can obtain a concerted movement at the time named it will doubtless be successful.

The main object of this letter is to state the time for the rising that it may be simultaneous over the whole South. To carry out the plan in the department in which you have the command, you are requested to select one or more intelligent contrabands, and, after telling them the plan and the time (night of the 1st of August), you will send them into the interior of the country within the enemy's lines and where the slaves are numerous, with instructions to communicate the plan and the time to as many intelligent slaves as possible, and requesting of each to circulate it far and wide over the country, so that we may be able to make the rising understood by several hundred thousand slaves by the time named.

When you have made these arrangements, please enclose this letter to some other General commanding in the same department with yourself, some one whom you know or believe to be favorable to such movement, and he, in turn, is requested to send it to another, and so on until it has traveled the entire round of the Department, and each command and post will in this way be acting together in the employment of Negro slaves to carry the plan into effect.

In this way, the plan will be adopted at the same time and in concert over the whole South, and yet no one of all engaged in it will learn the names of his associates, and will only know the number of Generals acting together in the movement. To give the last information, and before enclosing this letter to some other general, put the numeral "1" after the word "approved" at the bottom of the sheet:

And when it has gone the rounds of the department, the person last receiving it will please enclose it to my address, that I may then know and communicate that this plan is being carried out at the same time.

Yours respectfully, your obedient servant, Augustus S. Montgomery.

Indorsement

Department of North Carolina Approved.

This letter declaring this plan was sent to the military, but the copy sent to the Federal Governor or General at New Bern, falling into the hands of the Confederates, the plan miscarried. Communicated to General Lee he wrote as follows:

R. E. Lee to Hon. Secy of War. May 2, 1863.

Sir: I have the honor to enclose you a copy of a letter forwarded to me on the 21st inst. by his Excellency Gov. Vance of N.C. Gov. Vance states that it is a copy of an original letter addressed to Gen. Foster, and recently taken in a Federal mail, captured by some of our troops in the State service. The Governor also says that he has not given publicity to the letter, a course which I have advised him that I consider prudent and judicious.

I have suggested to Gov. Vance to cause the State and military authorities to be confidentially advised of the proposed movement, that proper precautionary measures may be adopted. Without knowing anything of the letter or the writer, further than may be inferred from the apparent indications of the connection of the latter either with those in authority or with others who have united to carry out this diabolical project, I deem it my duty to lay the matter before you for such action as you may see fit to take in the premises.

R.E. Lee, General.

(Official Records, Series 1, Vol. XVIII, pp. 1072-1073)

Such an insurrection, arranged for by the Government, was exactly what the people of the South apprehended when they withdrew from the Union. The apprehension was that the John Browns would give trouble and inaugurate a race war. It was feared that the Government would not seek to prevent John Brown insurrections, and, the better to guard against them, the Cotton States withdrew from the Union. The proposed general uprising of the African slaves speaks for itself.

Both in his proclamation of July 7th, 1864, and his second Inaugural, March 4th, 1865, Lincoln advocated a war, to last if necessary for conquest, till the South was "utterly destroyed." And Charles Francis Adams, the eminent Northern scholar and historian, says that the accepted policy of Lincoln's government during the last stages of hostilities was that there must be no humanity in war. (Adams, Studies, Military and Diplomatic, p. 266; Lee's Centennial, p. 53.) In line, were the oft quoted words and actions of Butler, Pope, Grant, Sherman and Sheridan. Nothing could be more extreme.

And to be sure, Northern writers would now be ashamed to record in history what their Northern friends had proposed as the fate of the Southern people. The question continually recurs—what had the South done to justify such a dreadful display of hate? Certainly the South had never done the North any harm. On the authority of Gen. E.D. Keyes in his Fifty Years' Observation of Men and Events, this hatred arose out of Southern monopoly of the offices and the general assumption

of "innate superiority" by Southerners in society and in Congress.

This hatred, or rather jealousy, of the South pursued it after the war, and no doubt accounted for the harshness of Reconstruction. There is an interesting letter in the correspondence of Andrew Johnson from Joseph S. Ingraham, long a druggist and apothecary and a leading citizen of Bangor, Maine, which is very full upon the subject. (See Tyler's Quarterly, XIV, pp. 9-10).

What great crime has the South ever committed against the North?... I say, why should those residing North of Mason and Dixon's Line so feel towards the inhabitants living South of it—and in a common country too?... I think it can be explained only on the ground of a feeling of jealousy on the part of the leading men of the North against a similar class South—for the genius and talent displayed by the latter on the floor of Congress and the influence heretofore exercised by her [the South] in the affairs of the government.

Well, Keyes had his wish, and now for seventy years the North has dominated the country. The South was whipped and thoroughly humiliated, slavery abolished, and its institutions assimilated to those of the North.

8. The Modern Case of John Brown

The parallel afforded by the cases of Sacco and Vanzeth to that of John Brown is too striking not to be noticed by the historian. At the dead of night on October 16, 1859, John Brown, whose hands were already red with innocent blood in Kansas, at the head of a band of desperate men, descended upon Harper's Ferry, with a view to start an insurrection of the slaves, and killed five persons, including a Negro who refused to join his band. There was no question of his guilt or the fairness of his trial, for he admitted both. He was condemned and executed.

Nevertheless, throughout the North and especially in the State of Massachusetts, sympathy with the murderer was manifested to an enormous extent, and modern historians, like Dr. Channing, have criticized Governor Henry A. Wise for not commuting his punishment. When war came shortly after, hastened by this unprecedented attack, it seemed as if the whole heart of the North beat in sympathy with John Brown, and no song was more popular than "John Brown's body lies a-mouldering in the grave, while his soul goes marching on."

The excuse for it all is that the people of the North chose to look to the end—the abolition of slavery—and came to a state of mind which justified in all its hideous and radical applications the false and immoral doctrine of "the end justifies the means."

The sober thought of the present hour in the North repudiates the madness of seventy years ago.

In the language, however, of the song "John Brown's soul marches on," it marched right on through the bloody war of the sixties, and remarkable to say, has marched on in our day, carrying murder and riot into the bosom of Massachusetts. The lawless soul of John Brown entered into two Italians—Sacco and Vanzeth.

Their cause was exactly the same as that of John Brown and his Abolitionists. Sacco and Vanzeth desired anarchy and the Abolitionist pronounced the Constitution "a covenant with death and an agreement with hell." The intelligentsia and intellectuals who flocked to Boston or joined in other lands in the protest to their execution had their exact parallel in Seward and Lincoln, who in speeches declared for the "higher law."

No doubt Sacco and Vanzeth had, like John Brown, an inspiration beyond their act, in which thousands like them have faith. They dreamed of an absolute freedom for man apart from laws which their fevered imaginations considered as made in the interest of the rich and the favored. No doubt, grievances exist in the status of Northern so-called "free labor," which borders close upon serfdom. They went to their death with the same intrepidity as characterized John Brown, but like him, they were murderers and law breakers. The end cannot justify the means. Ills in

society should be left to the curative power of education and the peaceful processes of discussion and resolve.

Governor Fuller of Massachusetts, like Henry A. Wise of Virginia, for refusing to interfere with the orderly administration of justice, was abused and threatened.

Demonstrations of sympathy with Sacco and Vanzeth exceeded those bestowed upon John Brown in 1856, but there was no yielding in the spirit of the Massachusetts authorities, although the case against Sacco and Vanzeth, being based upon circumstantial evidence, was nothing like as strong as the evidence against John Brown.

It was argued in Brown's case that his execution would make ten Abolitionists where only one existed before. And it may be that the execution of Sacco and Vanzeth may make twenty anarchists where only two existed before. But justice should not be deterred by such considerations.

The interesting fact, as far as history is concerned, is the marked inconsistency afforded in the conduct of Massachusetts. It ought, at least, to convey a lesson to her and all others that interference in the affairs of another State in the orderly administration of justice is a very improper thing.

The able paper of Paul S. Whitcomb in the last issue has the following wise utterance "The problems of the present are largely the legacy of the past, and if the past had settled them right, they would not confront us at the present time." The bloody and violent way in which the South was treated in the matter of slavery rises up to confront the North in the present extensive anarchical, communistic, and socialistic elements which threaten destruction to her society. John Brown's soul marches on!

This above is by Dr. Tyler.

There was a convention held by the Negroes of North Carolina on the 29th of September 1865. That convention declared: "Born upon the same soil and brought up in an intimacy of relationship unknown in any other State of Society, we have formed attachments for the White race which must be as enduring as life."

9. Why South Carolina Seceded

How came Secession? For years the Democrats had been in control of the Federal Government. The opposite party of former days, the Whig Party, had really passed away. The old Abolition faction at the North had adopted the name of the Republican party and had largely absorbed the Whigs of the North. The tariff issue of former days was now unheard of. The gold of California and cotton crops of the South had brought unheard of prosperity. But the Abolitionists of the North were disregarding the Constitution and the acts of Congress relating to slavery, and were so blackguarding and vilifying the slave holders, and threatening them with Negro insurrection that sectional animosity ran high in the homes of the people.

Yet the Democratic party was two to one compared to the Republicans, and their public men were looking forward to a long control of the Government.

There was not a suggestion to the contrary. But when the Democratic Convention met at Charleston in 1860, there arose a division that led to two Democratic nominees splitting the party and putting the election in jeopardy. Still it was said that if no election, the House of Representatives will certainly choose a Democrat for President. There was no thought of a Republican being elected President.

South Carolina chose electors for the Electoral College on election day—by its legislature—so the South Carolina legislature was in session on election day; and when the result of the election at the North was announced by telegraph it was astounding. So many Northern States, previously Democratic, had split their tickets that the Republican candidate was elected President. The popular vote was 4,680,703. Lincoln, receiving 1,860,452, was declared elected, he getting one hundred and eighty electoral votes at the

North, and Douglas only twelve; while Breckenridge got seventy-two electoral votes at the South. That result was appalling.

The legislature of South Carolina, being in session, called for a State Convention, which, on its meeting, passed an Ordinance of Secession, and then made "A Declaration of the Immediate Causes Which Induce and Justify the Secession of South Carolina from the Federal Union."

After the statement of some historical facts this Declaration continues:

Thus were established the two great principles asserted by the Colonies, namely: The right of a State to govern itself, and the right of a people to abolish a Government when it becomes destructive of the ends for which it was instituted. And concurrent with the establishment of these principles, was the fact that each Colony became, and was recognized by the mother Country as a Free, Sovereign, and Independent State.

Then it set forth the adoption of the Constitution by the people of each State, and:

Thus was established, by compact between the States, a government, with defined objects and powers, limited to the express words of the grant. This limitation left the whole remaining mass of power subject to the clause reserving it to the States or to the people, and rendered unnecessary any specification of reserved rights. We hold that the Government thus established is subject to the two great principles asserted in the Declaration of Independence; and we hold further, that the mode of its formation subjects it to a third fundamental principle, namely; the law of compact. We maintain that in every compact between two or more parties, the obligation is mutual; that the failure of one of the contracting parties to perform a material part of the agreement entirely releases the obligation of the other; and that where no arbiter is provided, each party is remitted to his own judgment to determine the fact of failure, with all its consequences.

In the present case, that fact is established with certainty. We assert that fourteen of the States have deliberately refused for years past to fulfill their constitutional obligations, and we refer to their own statutes for the proof.

The Constitution of the United States, in its 4th Article, provides as follows: "No person held to service or labor in one State, under the laws thereof, escaping into another shall, in consequence of any law or regulation therein, be discharged from service or labor, but shall be delivered up on claim of the party to whom such service or labor may be due."

This stipulation was so material to the compact that without it that compact would not have been made. The greater number of the contracting parties held slaves, and they had previously evinced their estimate of the value of such stipulation by making it a condition in the ordinance for the government of the territory ceded by Virginia, which now composes the States north of the Ohio river.

The same article of the Constitution stipulates also for rendition by the several States of fugitives from justice from the other States.

The General Government, as the common agent, passed laws to carry into effect these stipulations of the States. For many years these laws were executed. But an increasing hostility on the part of the non-slaveholding States to the institution of slavery has led to a disregard of their obligations, and the laws of the General Government have ceased to effect the objects of the Constitution. The States of Maine, New Hampshire, Vermont, Massachusetts, Connecticut, Rhode Island, New York, Pennsylvania, Illinois, Indiana, Michigan, Wisconsin and Iowa, have enacted laws which either nullify the Acts of Congress or render useless any attempt to execute them. In many of these States the fugitive is discharged from the service or labor claimed, and in none of them has the

State government complied with the stipulation made in the Constitution. The State of New Jersey, at an early day, passed a law in conformity with her constitutional obligation; but the current of antislavery feeling has led her more recently to enact laws which render inoperative the remedies provided by her own law and by the laws of Congress. In the State of New York even the right of transit for a slave has been denied by her tribunals; and the States of Ohio and Iowa have refused to surrender to justice fugitives charged with murder and with inciting servile insurrection in the State of Virginia. Thus the constitutional compact has

been deliberately broken and disregarded by the non-slaveholding States, and the consequence follows that South Carolina is released from her obligation.

The ends for which this Constitution was framed are declared by itself to be "to form a more perfect union, establish justice, insure domestic tranquility, provide for the common defense, promote the general welfare, and secure the blessings of liberty to ourselves and our posterity."

These ends it endeavored to accomplish by a Federal Government, in which each State was recognized as an equal and had separate control over its own institutions. The right of property in slaves was recognized by giving to free persons distinct political rights, by giving them the right to representation, and burthening them with direct taxes for three-fifths of their slaves; by authorizing the importation of slaves for twenty years, and by stipulating for the rendition of fugitives from labor.

We affirm that these ends for which this Government was instituted have been defeated, and the Government itself has been made destructive of them by the action of the non-slaveholding States. Those States have assumed the right of deciding upon the propriety of our domestic institutions, and have denied the rights of property established in fifteen of the States, and recognized by the Constitution; they have denounced as sinful the institution of slavery; they have permitted the open establishment among them of societies whose avowed purpose is to disturb the peace and to eloign the property of the citizens of other States. They have encouraged and assisted thousands of our slaves to leave their homes; and those who remain, have been incited by emissaries, books, and pictures to servile insurrection.

For twenty-five years this agitation has been steadily increasing until it has now secured to its aid the power of the Common Government. Observing the forms of the Constitution, a sectional party has found within that article establishing the Executive Department the means of subverting the Constitution itself. A geographical line has been drawn across the Union, and all the States North of that line have united in the election of a man to the high office of President of the United States whose opinions and purposes are hostile to slavery. He is to be entrusted with the administration of the Common Government because he has declared that that "Government cannot endure permanently half slave, half free," and that the public mind must rest in the belief that slavery is in the course of ultimate extinction.

This sectional combination for the subversion of the Constitution has been aided in some of the States by elevating to citizenship persons, who, by the Supreme Law of the land, are incapable of becoming citizens; and their votes have been used to inaugurate a new policy, hostile to the South and destructive to its peace and safety.

On the 4th of March next, this party will take possession of the Government. It has announced that the South shall be excluded from the common territory; that the Judicial Tribunals shall be made sectional, and that a war must be waged against slavery until it shall cease throughout the United States.

The Guaranties of the Constitution will then no longer exist; the equal rights of the States will be lost. The slaveholding States will no longer have the power of self-government or selfprotection, and the Federal Government will have become their enemy.

Sectional interest and animosity will deepen the irritation, and all hope of remedy is rendered vain by the fact that public opinion at the North has invested a great political error with the sanction of a more erroneous religious belief.

We, therefore, the people of South Carolina, by our delegates, in Convention assembled, appealing to the Supreme Judge of the world for the rectitude of our intentions, have solemnly declared that the Union heretofore existing between this State and the other States of North America is dissolved, and that the State of South Carolina has resumed her position among the nations of the world as a separate and independent State, with full power to levy war, conclude peace, contract alliances, establish commerce, and to do all other acts and things which independent States may of right do.

Senator Clingman, of North Carolina, on the secession of the Gulf States, told the Senators that this action was because they believed that "Mr. Lincoln, elected President, was a dangerous man." He had already declared that "the Union could not exist half free and half slave," although slavery had existed in it from its formation, and there was no reason for any change. He had no regard for the Constitution in his acts as President, and but little for his statement of facts. He proved to be a dangerous man and without regard to the happiness of the people North and South. Never was there such a horrible besom of destruction as Abraham Lincoln inaugurated in our Christian country.

10. Secession of the Cotton States

In a general way, history speaks of the secession of the Southern States as being an incident of slavery. Seven States seceded in the winter of 1860, and on March 11, 1861, formed a new Confederacy with virtually the same Constitution. The other Southern States seceded later when called on to engage in a war against this new Confederacy. Why was that first secession? Had there been no Africans held in slavery, there might have been no secession. African slavery had existed in every colony and State, and was particularly recognized and cared for in the Constitution, every State agreeing to return to the owner any fugitive slave.

In time, the Northern States abandoned slavery. Still every man who held office swore to support the Constitution under which Congress has to provide for the general welfare of the United States, and has to make all laws necessary and proper (Article 1, Sec. 8).

At length the Abolition sentiment grew at the North, so much so that some persons there wished to abolish slavery in the Southern States; and, to bring that about, they promoted Negro revolt and insurrections. Thus it came about that a joint committee of the two Houses of the Legislature in North Carolina, in 1831, reported they were satisfied "that an extensive combination now exists to excite in the minds of the slaves and colored persons of this and other slave States feelings and opinions leading to insurrections." They also reported "the actual detection of the circulation of the incendiary publications and discovery of the designs," etc., "and we are led to fear the most ruinous consequences." (This was in 1831).

While Nat Turner's insurrection occurred in Virginia, a similar attempt was made near Wilmington, N.C. After that, year by year, Abolition sentiment continued to grow at the North until, at length, a dozen Northern States nullified the Constitution and

Acts of Congress, and, in Massachusetts, even burned them! It was declared that these States "have permitted the open establishment of societies whose avowed object is to disturb the peace of other States." "They have incited by emissaries, books, and pictures the Negroes to servile insurrection."

In 1857, a defamatory book was written. The Impending Crisis, and at the election of 1858, it was endorsed by the Republican Congressmen and widely circulated throughout the North. Its effect was notable. That party increased its membership in Congress from sixty-seven to nearly double that number. In it the author said to the slave-holders:

Henceforth, Sirs, we are demandants—not suppliants. It is for you to decide whether we are to have justice peaceably or by violence. For whatever consequences may follow, we are determined to have it one way or another. Would you be instrumental in bringing upon yourselves, your wives, and your children a fate too terrific to contemplate? Shall history cease

to cite as an instance of unexampled cmelty the massacre of St. Bartholomew because the World —the South—shall have furnished a more direful scene of atrocity and carnage?

Such was the picture of slaughter proposed by the fanatic Abolitionists.

Then John Brown, after raising a considerable sum of money in Boston and elsewhere and obtaining a supply of arms, on Sunday, October 16, 1859, started on his mission. With a force of seventeen Whites and five Negroes, he captured the arsenal at Harper's Ferry, expecting the slaves to rise and begin the massacre of the White slaveholders. The military was able to prevent that, and Brown was tried and executed. Then, throughout the North, John Brown was said to have gone straight to heaven—a saint!

In the Senate, Stephen A. Douglas, pursuant to the Constitution, introduced a bill to punish those people who seek to incite slave insurrections. "Abraham Lincoln, in his speech at New York, declared it was a seditious speech"—"His press and party hooted it." "It received their jeers and jibes." (See Stephen's Pictorial History, p. 663).

When Congress met on the fifth day of December, 1859, the Republicans proposed John Sherman for Speaker. Thereupon, some Democrats offered a resolution that no man who indorsed Helper's Impending Crisis was fit to be Speaker. That raised such a conflict that a riot ensued, the members carrying pistols; and it was not until February 22 that the House organized by electing as Speaker an old line Whig. The House would not approve Negro insurrections after a conflict lasting more than two months.

Then came the election of President. The party of Negro insurrections swept the Northern States. The people of the South had realized the possible results. With the people and the State Governments of the North making a saint out of a man who had planned and started to murder the slaveholders—the Whites of the South—and the Northern States all going in favor of that party which protected those engaged in such plans, naturally there were in every Southern State those who thought it best to guard against such massacres by separating from those States where John Brown was deified.

When the news came that Lincoln was elected, the South Carolina Legislature, being in session, called a State Convention. When the Convention met, it withdrew from the Union. In its declaration it said: "Those States have encouraged and assisted thousands of our slaves to leave their homes; and those who remain have been incited by emissaries, books, and pictures to servile insurrection. For twenty-five years this agitation has been steadily increasing, until it has now secured to its aid the power of the common government." So, to escape insurrections, South Carolina began the secession movement. And there was good cause to seek safety by withdrawing from Lincoln's Government. He was not opposed to the Negro massacre of the Southern people.

At the last of August, 1862, General Pope, who was in command of the army near Washington, was defeated, and, in September, President Lincoln thought that by threatening to free the Negroes at the South he might help his prospects in the war. Delegations from the churches in Chicago also addressed him. He said he hesitated. It was to be a war measure. There were those who deemed it a barbarity to start an insurrection of the Negroes. As to that, President Lincoln

said: "Nor do I urge objections of a moral nature in view of possible consequences of insurrection and massacre at the South."

The French newspaper at New York said: "Does the Government at Washington mean to say that, on January 1st, it will call for a servile war to aid in the conquest of the South? And after the Negroes have killed the Whites, the Negroes themselves must be drowned in their own blood."

Many other newspapers asked the same question. But Mr. Lincoln contented himself with what he had said. Governor Morton of Indiana was for the insurrection! Charles Sumner in his Speech at Faneuil Hall said of the Southern slaveholders: "When they rose against a paternal government, they set an example of insurrection. They cannot complain if their slaves, with better reason, follow it." And so the North was for the insurrection!

At length, in May, 1863, it was arranged that there should be a general insurrection throughout the South, as the following discloses (letter reproduced on pp. 56-57).

This letter declaring this plan was sent to the military, but the copy sent to the Federal Governor or General at New Bern, falling into the hands of the Confederates, the plan miscarried. Such an insurrection, arranged for by the Government, was not exactly what the people of the South apprehended when they withdrew from the Union. The apprehension was that the John Browns would give trouble and inaugurate a race war. It was feared that the Government would not seek to prevent John Brown insurrections, and the better to guard against them, the cotton States withdrew from the Union. The proposed general uprising of the African slaves speaks for itself.

11. President Lincoln's Inaugural

In the Veteran, I sought to show the right of the Cotton States to withdraw from the Union. That right was denied by Mr. Lincoln. In his first Inaugural, he said:

A disruption of the Federal Union, heretofore only menaced, is now formidably attempted. I hold that in contemplation of universal law and of the Constitution, the Union of these States is perpetual. Perpetuity is implied, if not expressed, in the fundamental law of all national governments. It is safe to assert that no government proper ever had a provision in its organic law for its own termination. Continue to execute all the express provisions of our national Constitution, and the Union will endure forever, it being impossible to destroy it except by some action not provided for in the instrument itself.

Again, if the United States be not a government proper, but an association of States, in the nature of contract merely, can it, as a contract, be peaceably unmade by less than all the parties who made it? One party to a contract may violate it—break it, so to speak—but does it not require all to lawfully rescind it?

Descending from these general principles, we find the proposition that in legal contemplation the Union is perpetual confirmed by the history of the Union itself. The Union is much older than the Constitution. It was formed, in fact, by the Articles of Association in 1774. It was matured and continued by the Declaration of Independence in 1776. It was further matured, and the faith of all the then thirteen States expressly plighted and engaged that it should be perpetual by the Articles of Confederation in 1778. And, finally, in 1787, one of the declared objects for ordaining and establishing the Constitution was "to form a more perfect Union."

But if destruction of the Union by one or by a part only of the States be lawfully possible, the Union is less perfect than before the Constitution, having lost the vital element of perpetuity.

It follows from these views that no State upon its own mere motion can lawfully get out of the Union; that resolves and ordinances to that effect are legally void, and that acts of violence within any State or States against the authority of the United States are insurrectionary or revolutionary, according to circumstances.

I therefore consider that, in view of the Constitution and the laws, the Union is unbroken, and to the extent of my ability I shall take care, as the Constitution itself expressly enjoins upon me, that all the laws of the Union be faithfully executed in all the States.

Mr. Lincoln, like a million of other boys, had but a limited education and entered on the

activities of life under such circumstances that it is said that he and his partner had a store with a license to sell liquor. He, however, began to practice law, and made a success of it—in the local courts.

12. Lincoln and the Constitution

In the present constitution of North Carolina, it is declared that the people of the State are a part of the American nation, and there is no right on the part of the State to secede; that every citizen owes paramount allegiance to the Constitution and Government of the United States; and all officers are sworn to support and maintain the constitution of the State.

So, North Carolinians, by law now, are all nationals. Still, history is history, and Lincoln said in a message to Congress: "Fellow citizens, we cannot escape history." In 1774, when each Colony was a separate entity with its own royal governor, and the people loyal subjects, the Continental Congress said to our king: "Your royal authority over us and our connections with Great Britain we shall always endeavor to support and maintain carefully and zealously."

However, the members of this Congress entered into a personal association to seek to have certain purposes accomplished, such as "nonimportation," "nonexportation," and they recommended that "in every county, city, and town, committees shall be chosen to observe the conduct of all persons touching this association." When a copy of this association paper was received in North Carolina, the members of the North Carolina convention personally agreed to stand by this association and to ask their constituents at home to do so. But the convention forbade the delegates in the Continental Congress to enter into any special agreement whatever for this colony without special authority to do so. The association was a mere personal affair, like the Masons. Whatever action was taken by the several Colonies in pursuance of the recommendations of the Continental Congress was the voluntary action of the Colonies.

Now, let us see what Mr. Lincoln says about that in his Inaugural. He says: 'The Union is much older than the Constitution. It was formed, in fact, by the Articles of Association in 1774."

So, he considered the association of some of the public men as a union of colonies, although the very men in North Carolina who went into the association forbade the North Carolina delegates to enter into any agreement whatever for this colony without special authority to do so, and there was no such agreement. So much for Mr. Lincoln's accuracy.

A year elapsed, and a new convention, under the changed conditions, invested the delegates with power to bind the province, in honor, by any act they do, and the convention resolved "to exert every influence to induce the inhabitants of North Carolina to observe the rules the Continental Congress shall recommend." But while there was this personal cooperation, as yet the provinces were not united in any union—some of the public men were in association to carry into effect the recommendations of the Continental Congress; and in July, 1775, the convention resolved that "the inhabitants of North Carolina should pay their full proportion of the expenses of maintaining

the army"- not the provinces, but the inhabitants.

And then there was considered a plan of union; but that plan was rejected, and there was no plan of union agreed on. So, things stood until 1776, the people being British subjects and protesting loyalty to their king. The Provinces were not united. Then came the Declaration of Independence, which was the concurring act of the several colonies. Each colony acted by its delegates especially commissioned to join in doing so. At first only twelve agreed. New York had not. So the Declaration of Independence, July 4, 1776, was signed by only twelve colonies. The instrument declared that each Province was "a free and Independent State with power to do anything that any other State could rightfully do."

Up to this time there was no union of the Provinces, but in 1777, a plan of union was prepared, and was submitted to each State for ratification. It was not to go into effect until ratified by every State.

Now, each Province called itself "a free, independent, sovereign State" without any superior at all. But they were all engaged in the common cause of making their claim of independence. The proposed Articles of Confederation were not finally accepted and did not go into effect until 1781. They read; "Articles of Confederation and perpetual unity between the States of (naming each State);" not over them, but "between" them. "The style of the Confederacy shall be the United States of America." The second article is: "Each State retains its sovereignty, freedom, and independence, and every power, jurisdiction, and right not expressly delegated by it." The third article is; "The said States hereby severally enter into a firm league of friendship with each other for their common defense to assist each other for their common defense to assist each other." In article thirteen, it is said; "And the Articles of this Confederation shall be inviolably observed by every State, and the Union shall be perpetual; nor shall any alteration at any time hereafter be made in any of them, unless such alterations be agreed to in a Congress of the United States and be afterwards confirmed by the legislature of every State."

Here, then, was a declaration of sovereignty in each State, and a league of friendship that was to be a perpetual Confederation, to be unchangeable except by consent of every State, each State retaining its sovereignty. The several States claimed to be sovereign from 1776. As such, these Articles of Confederation, so declaring, were agreed to by some in 1777 and 1778, but Maryland did not ratify them, and they were not in force until 1781. In the meantime all the States were sovereign States. This league of friendship was ratified in 1781, and then went into operation. It was the first agreement for union, and the Union was a confederation of sovereign States. This was followed by the Treaty of Peace with Great Britain in which "His Britannic Majesty, acknowledging the said United States—viz.: Massachusetts, South Carolina, North Carolina (naming each State), to be free, sovereign, and independent States, treats with them as such," etc. —treating with each State as a separate sovereignty. Other treaties were likewise made with the several States, naming each State that was in the Confederation. So the Confederation of sovereign States went into effect. At length in 1787, it was proposed to amend these Articles of Confederation and a convention was called, its report to be submitted to every State for its ratification. The Constitution proposed by this convention differed from the Articles of Confederation in several points. First, it was not declared to be a perpetual Union of the States; and, second, it was to go into effect between any nine that ratified it, leaving the other States out. Whatever union had had existed between the States accepting this new Constitution and those

not accepting it was to be ignored. Then there was an omission of the declaration of the sovereignty of each State. This omission was not unnatural. Each State knew that it was a sovereign State, and there was no occasion for asserting it. The inhabitants in every State knew that their State and all other States were sovereign States, and so that was not mentioned. They were States from 1776, and not in any union up to 1781. Suppose Maryland had not ratified the Confederation, and the proposed Articles of Confederation had not gone into effect; when peace had come, what would have been the relation of the separate, free, independent, sovereign State, as acknowledged by all the nations, and claimed by each State? They had only the tie of friendship.

Nor was there a declaration in the proposed Constitution that Congress had only the powers delegated to it; the States retaining all powers not delegated. That likewise was so plain that it was not then asserted. Eventually, the Constitution was ratified by eleven States.

New York, noticing the omission mentioned above, in her ratification "did declare and make known that all power is originally vested in and subsequently derived from the people... that the powers of government may be resumed by the people; that every power, jurisdiction, and right which is not only by this Constitution clearly delegated to the Congress of the United States, remains to the people of the several States."

Virginia, in her ratification likewise said that the people of the several States could resume the powers delegated. The Continental Congress, with these ratifications before it, said that they were sufficient, and declared the Constitution ratified, provided for the election of the President and started the new Government. North Carolina and Rhode Island had not ratified the Constitution. So the new Union became operative in 1789 between eleven States, two not being in the Union.

What was the situation of Rhode Island and North Carolina when the other States broke up the old Confederation and began the new Union? The old Union, designed to be perpetual, was gone, and these two States were sovereign States alone in the world. While the United States Congress made its new laws about commerce. North Carolina and Rhode Island made their own laws. We here in North Carolina knew that, in 1788, North Carolina was a free, sovereign, independent State. We made our own laws and governed ourselves, and there was no legal connection with any other State.

In framing the Constitution, as some of the powers which the States delegated to the Congress (similar to those delegated in the Articles of Confederation), were national in their nature, the word "national" was freely used in the first draft of the instrument, but as the States were not forming a nation, but only making a more perfect Union of the Confederation, the word "national" was entirely eliminated; a nation was not to be created—only a sisterhood of States united in Union which had national powers. It was "between the States," not over them—so declared in its last article. By virtue of their sovereignty, eleven States withdrew from the perpetual Union.

Quickly after Congress met a dozen amendments of the Constitution were submitted to the States —one being to supply the omission of the declaration that the States retain all rights not delegated, just as New York and Virginia had mentioned; and it was adopted.

The States had long been acknowledged as sovereign States, and as sovereign States they had formed the Union of the United States in the Confederacy. Now, as sovereign States they were forming a more perfect Union, and there was no need to assert that they were sovereign States any more than Great Britain should declare that she was a sovereign State. They possessed all rights not delegated, and Congress had only such of the sovereign powers of the sovereign States as they had each delegated, retaining all other sovereign powers of each State.

Now, see what Mr. Lincoln says in his message of July 4, 1861:

Our States have neither more nor less power than that reserved to them in the Union by the Constitution, no one of them ever having been a State out of the Union. The original ones passed into the Union even before they cast off their British colonial dependence. Having never been States, either in substance or in name, outside the Union, whence this magical omnipotence of State rights, asserting a claim of power to lawfully destroy the Union itself?... Much is said about the sovereignty of the States, but the word even is not in the national Constitution, nor, as is believed, in any of the State constitutions. Would it be far wrong to define it: sovereignty, political community without a political superior? Tested by this, none of our States, except Texas, ever was a sovereignty. The States have their status in the Union, and they have no other legal status.

Such was Lincoln's philosophy, ignoring plain facts of history.

Now, thirteen sovereign States had formed the perpetual Confederacy. Eleven of them withdrew from that "perpetual unchangeable Union" and adopted the new Constitution. They withdrew in virtue of their sovereignty, and it was declared without objection that "the people of any State could resume the powers delegated." Senator Lodge, in his Life of Webster, says: "It is safe to say that there was not a man in the country, from Washington and Hamilton to Clinton and Mason, who did not regard the new system as an experiment from which each and every State had a right to peaceably withdraw." Indeed, the right to withdraw was so generally accepted that it was later taught in the textbook at the Military Academy at West Point. Certainly, it was a power of a sovereign State.

Eleven States withdrew from the perpetual Confederation, and North Carolina and Rhode Island were left alone in the world. But here we have President Lincoln declaring that the States were not sovereign, that, while subjects of the king, they formed a Union which is supreme over the people of the States: that no State ever existed outside the Union, and people of the States cannot govern themselves outside of the Union.

And so, without any authorization by Congress, he began a war on the Southern States. A few months after he began it, he had Congress to meet, and the first thing offered in the Senate was a resolution confirming and legalizing his acts, as if they had been authorized. This particular resolution was before the Senate fifteen times between July 6 and August 6, and was never passed. Then, after twenty months of warfare, the Supreme Court of the United States (67 U. S. Reports, page 668), said Congress had no power delegated to it to make war upon a State, and that the President had no authority to make war. That "the Civil War between the Northern and Southern States arose because the citizens of the States owed a supreme allegiance to the United States which the Southern States sought to absolve them from, by State secession, and the right

of a State to do that was now being decided by wager of battle."

There was no reason or ground stated to justify the claim that "the citizens of each State owned a supreme allegiance to the United States." It was a war by the Northern States to hold the Southern States in union with them; a conquest of free, sovereign, and independent States to be held under the domination of the more numerous States. Senator Baker, of Oregon, declared in the Senate that he favored "reducing the population of the Southern States to abject subjection to the sway of the government." "We may have to reduce the Southern States to the condition of territories, and send them from Massachusetts or from Illinois, governors to control them. I would do that." (Globe LW, page 48). Such was the spirit of those who made the war. President Lincoln said: "Fellow citizens, we cannot escape history."

The last article of the Constitution reads: "The ratifications of the convention of nine States shall be sufficient for the establishment of this Constitution between the States so ratifying the same.

The Declaration of Independence says: "The united colonies are and of right ought to be free and independent States."

Then, in 1788, after the Constitution had been ratified by eleven States, North Carolina and Rhode Island not assenting, the election of President was held by the eleven States and George Washington was the first President.

It is to be observed that Abraham Lincoln says that no State ever was a State out of the Union: and that the Union was made in 1774. All untrue! He did not know what he was talking about!!

13. Lincoln the Lawyer

A story is told of Lincoln, the lawyer.

In trying a case, a witness narrated what he saw at night. Lincoln examined that witness and questioned how he could have observed that at night. The witness replied it was moonlight. Lincoln in speaking to the jury held up a printed almanac and read from it that there was no moonlight on that particular night—and the statement is that he read from an almanac of the previous year, not of the night of the occurrence!

The fact has been denied, but its popular acceptance shows that Lincoln could not have been thought over-scrupulous by people who knew him. According to his friends, Lincoln's tactics in the Legislature were of a very similar order. He log rolled and traded in the offices, and there is a story which has never been denied of his joining with others in tricking a Democratic paper into publishing an article which Lincoln, himself, was foremost in denouncing after the publication. (Herndon, Vol. II, p. 370).

He was a past master at uttering sophisms. When he prepared his Inaugural of March 4, 1861, he announced that "no State could withdraw from the Union." To sustain that position he said: "The Union is much older than the Constitution. It was formed in fact by the 'Articles of Association' in 1774. It was matured and continued by the Declaration of Independence in 1776. It was further matured by the Articles of Confederation in 1778, and finally in 1788 the Constitution formed a more perfect Union."

The lawyer slipped up when he mentioned the Articles of 1774. There was an association to prohibit the importation of goods, but it was in no sense a political union. It is ridiculous to say that the colonies entered the Union then when they were telling the King of England how much they loved him, as they did at that time.

The lawyer cites the Articles of 1778. Again, there were no articles of 1778. Some had been proposed, to go into effect when all of the States should have agreed to these Articles. They went into effect in 1781. The Union was to be perpetual, and the Articles were never to be changed except by the consent of every State. But in a few years the wish was for "a more perfect Union." The old Articles were cast aside, and a new compact was agreed to by eleven States, but it said nothing about perpetuity as the old did. They elected their Congress and their President. How about the two that did not agree to it? The lawyer says "there never was a State out of the Union except Texas." How about North Carolina and Rhode Island in 1789? Not in the Union at all! A bill passed by the Senate treated Rhode Island as a foreign State and forbade all importations from her.

The lawyer stands from under—when Virginia, New York and Rhode Island in their several acceptances of the proposed Constitution declared that the people of each State shall have the right to withdraw the State from the Union. Washington and everybody assented to that. Indeed, secession was taught at West Point, and Senator Lodge in his Life of Webster says: "It is safe to say that there was not a man in the country who did not regard the new system as an experiment from which every State had a right to withdraw."

Why did he start the war? Nicolay & Hay, close to Mr. Lincoln as brothers, writing as of April 1, 1861, p. 442, Vol. III, said: "When the President determined on war, and with the purpose of making it appear that the South was the aggressor, he took measures," etc.

Nevertheless, he asserted that "slavery was the cause of the war." "And to strengthen, perpetuate and extend it was the object for which the insurgents would rend the Union even by war."

The lawyer speaks and holds up the wrong almanac! It was the intemperate agitation in the North against slavery, the refusal to submit to the decision of the Supreme Court in reference to the territories, and the instigation to massacre encouraged through many years that caused secession. But secession was not war. Norway seceded from Sweden and there was no war. It was Lincoln that made war. North Carolina and Virginia and some other States were still in the Union, and he called on then to join him in his war! They refused and stood with the South. As to South Carolina, who seceded first, where was she going "to extend slavery?" In the sea? So likewise, the other Southern States, where could they extend slavery after secession? He attributes starting the war to the Southern States, and then, behold, he attributes his own actions to the Creator!

Early in 1865, President Davis asked President Lincoln to cease his battles and permit the people of the Southern States to return their States to the Union. Lincoln had already proclaimed the freedom of every slave in the South. And the decree had been accepted. Had he now agreed to let the Southern States exercise domestic power as of old, the South would have come back.

In response to this request, President Lincoln said "No, Southerners must surrender unconditionally before the war should cease," and thereby he became responsible for Reconstruction and all its attendant horrors. In his second Inaugural he ascribes his action to the Great Lord of Heaven, "If God wills it to continue, etc."

14. Lincoln's Inhumanity

One of the first acts of Lincoln, after declaring war, was to declare Confederate privateersmen pirates, subject to death. This doctrine was contrary to the practice of the Americans in the war of the Revolution, and was denounced in the British Parliament as nothing short of legalizing murder. President Davis threatened retaliation, and Lincoln, justly humiliated, desisted. Another of his first acts after declaring war was to proclaim all medicines contraband of war. Civilized warfare had been confined to military operations, but President Lincoln sought to promote the death of women and children in their homes. That was similar to the deification of John Brown for seeking to have the Africans massacre the women of the South.

With the applause of President Lincoln, his generals, invading the country where there were only women and children, caused devastation and desolation. Vattel teaches that private property on land is not to be taken in war unless paid for. But this humane rule was totally neglected by his soldiers. Grant, Sherman, Pope, Hunter and Sheridan boasted of their destructive conduct.

Then in regard to the treatment of prisoners, Lincoln was equally indifferent to the requirements of civilization. At first, there was an exchange of prisoners, but later that was forbidden. There were many held on each side. As Lincoln had declared medicines contraband of war, Davis asked for permission to buy at the North medicines for the Northern prisoners, but his request was refused. In the meantime, great numbers of Southern soldiers were dying in Northern prisons: Lincoln would not exchange. At length. President Davis offered to parole 15,000 sick Northern soldiers and let them go North if Lincoln would send ships to take them away. After a long delay, Lincoln sent the ships and carried the fifteen thousand to their homes and then later, he sent about three thousand five hundred Confederate sick men to the South, of whom five hundred died on the voyage. Although the South was denied medicines, many more Confederates, being prisoners, died at the North than Northern prisoners died at the South. Undoubtedly Lincoln's cutting down the rations of Confederate prisoners twenty per cent contributed to this.

Then after declining to cease his battles, and let the Southern States return to the Union, if they would do so, he proposed to continue the war to the last extremity, saying:

Yet if God wills that it continues until all the wealth piled by the bondsman's two hundred and fifty years of unrequited toil shall be sunk, and until every drop of blood drawn with the lash shall be paid by another drawn with the sword, as was said three thousand years ago, still it must be said. The judgments of the Lord are true and righteous altogether.

This is the message in which he spoke of "charity to all and malice to none," but where is the

charity in this passage? In this passage the slave owner is described as an incarnate demon, and the Lord very unjustly held responsible for Lincoln's own determinations. Was Washington a devil, was Jefferson one, was Lee one? They were all slave owners.

Now on the 22nd of December, 1862, when Lincoln's war had been in progress eighteen months, the Supreme Court of the United States in a case before it, mentioned that "under the Constitution Congress had no right to make war on any State, and that the President had no right to make any war." It mentioned the war then in progress as "one between the Northern and Southern States." It was not a rebellion, but it was not "a war between the States." Lincoln had asked the States no odds, and it was Lincoln's war against the Southern States; a Grand Invasion. And five months after the decision of the Supreme Court, it was arranged that on the 16th of August, 1863, the Negroes from Virginia to Texas should, with the aid of the Northern generals in the South, rise in insurrection—a measure contemplating the murder of the defenseless women and children of the South by the Africans! Whether Lincoln knew of this conspiracy cannot be shown, but it was in conformity with his bloody message above cited. This, however, miscarried and the war went on until the North had conquered the South and reduced the sovereign States of the South to mere provinces of the North.

The great sin of Lincoln and the Northern agitators in general was by constant agitation to identify slavery with the pride of the South, and to prevent any steps being taken toward abolishing it. With independence, the South would have been free of these irritating and disgusting interferences, murders and assassinations.

Society in general has its unity of resemblances in all nations. Civilized people in all climes tend to wear the same kind of hats, and the same kind of clothes, and an independent South would have conformed to the ideas of the world at large. Slavery would have been abolished in a manner less hurtful to the South, naturally and peacefully, and in the meantime the South would have advanced in all the elements of prosperity.

Another example of Lincoln's inhumanity is to be found in his approval of the acts of his officials in arresting and confining in loathsome dungeons thousands of people in the North on bare suspicion of sympathy with the South. Old men of seventy were dragged from their beds at midnight and hurried to prison by squads of soldiers. When a prominent Democrat, C.L. Vallandigham, was arrested and tried by a military tribunal and sentenced to close confinement during the war, Lincoln, while changing the punishment to banishment, wrote a letter approving the policy of such arrests. Under this system of military trials in places where the courts were wide open, Capt. Henry Wirz and Mrs. Surratt were condemned and executed. Finally, after the war had ended the case of Lamdin P. Milligan, who had been sentenced to death by a military court, reached the United States Supreme Court, and then that court released the prisoner and decided that "martial rule is confined to the locality of actual war and can never exist in places where the courts are open and in the proper and unobstructed exercise of their jurisdiction." (Wallace Reports, p. 2).

Having begun hostilities against the seceded States, President Lincoln quickly declared that medicines were contraband—and so he thought to bring about the death of sick people at the South—the women and children. He went so far that he refused to allow the authorities of the South to purchase medicines at the North, to be used by Northern physicians and given to the

Northern soldiers who had been taken prisoners.

15. Lincoln the Usurper

In the political campaign of 1858, the sixty-four members of Congress who belonged to the Republican party, by endorsing Helper's book, The Impending Crisis, doubled their numbers elected to Congress; and at the Presidential election, elected Abraham Lincoln as President. His election by the adherents of John Brown and Negro insurrections led the Southern States to consider that he was a dangerous man to be President, and the people of South Carolina, to escape Negro insurrections, withdrew from the Union. Six other Southern States likewise withdrew, and in February 1861 organized the Southern Confederacy. Congress was in session and James Buchanan was President.

They did not protest against it. The Northern people were about equally divided as to the right of a State to withdraw from the Union. Neither Congress nor President Buchanan took any step against it. But Congress passed a measure to amend the Constitution that, it was hoped, would lead the seceded States to return.

When a member of Congress in 1847, Mr. Lincoln had made a speech declaring that "the people of any State have a right to withdraw from any Union." But now that the States had withdrawn because he had been elected President, they considering that he was "a dangerous man," it was a personal matter with Lincoln.

When he was inaugurated, on March 4, 1861, he stated in his Inaugural, that, "The States had no right to secede;" and he was led to declare that the Southern States were in rebellion, and that "it was his duty to enforce the laws in those States."

So many of the Northern people were indifferent about the matter that Lincoln thought it would be well to stir them up by having the Southern people to fire on the flag of the Union. So he arranged to bring that about, and he started a war about the middle of April, and he called on all the States for troops, and on the people to join his armies.

Now the Constitution gives to Congress the right to make war, but it does not give that right to the President.

However, he did not submit the matter to Congress until July. July 4, was a day of patriotism, and he called Congress to meet on this day, and in his message to Congress he detailed what he had done, in suppressing the "insurrection," as he called the action of the Southern States in leaving the "Union."

He said, "These measures, whether strictly legal or not were ventured upon under what appeared

to be a popular demand and public necessity, trusting then as now that Congress would readily ratify them." "It is believed that nothing has been done beyond the constitutional competency of Congress." (Messages of the Presidents, Vol. VI, p. 24).

So here was a statement that he knew that he was exceeding his powers in starting that war; and that he was usurping the powers of Congress. But Congress passed no measures approving of what President Lincoln had done.

Although such a resolution was up before Congress many times before Congress adjourned, it was never passed.

Indeed, as a matter of fact, Congress itself had no right to make war on one of the States.

So many of the Northern people thought that the Southern people had done only what they had a right to do, that Congress would not approve of what the President had done. He was a usurper of powers he did not have, as President. And at the North, there were those who called him a tyrant.

Theodore Roosevelt in a speech at Grand Rapids, September 8, 1900, said that in 1864, "on every hand Lincoln was denounced as a tyrant, a shedder of blood, a foe to liberty, a would-be dictator, a founder of an empire." (See Minor, The Real Lincoln, page 87).

Joe Parker, Professor of Law in Harvard, said: "Do you not perceive that the President is not only an absolute monarch but that his is an absolutely uncontrollable government, a perfect military despotism?"

It is to be recorded that the anti-war spirit in some parts of the North ran so high that on the 19th of August, 1863, President Lincoln issued a proclamation suspending the privileges of the writ of habeas corpus throughout the Union, and many thousands of citizens were arrested.

At the Presidential election in 1864 many of the soldiers were not allowed to vote against him but the vote stood 1,800,000 against him and only 2,213,000 for him. The North was far from being united for him.

Indeed, we may say that the Democratic party at the North as well as some others were for peace with the South; and had not McClellan, the Democratic nominee in 1864, said that he would carry on the war, better than Lincoln, instead of standing for peace he would have been elected and the war would have ended with recognition of the Southern Confederacy.

There is no question but that the usurper was a most unusual despot. We have observed that the President admitted disregarding the Constitution that he had taken oath to obey and usurping the power vested only in Congress. His purpose was to have his own way without regard to others or to his oath of office. So later, when President Davis and our Vice President Stephens, and others, at the meeting at Hampton Roads, begged him to stop the war and let the people of the Southern States return their States to the Union, he said "No." "Submit to me, the war must go on." And that meant more deaths to the soldiers—more horrible conditions to the children and women of both the South and the North.

Not only was he the usurper, but one of the most terrible tyrants in history. His General, William

T. Sherman, said, "War is Hell," and some of the Federal Generals and President Lincoln made it so. Not only was Lincoln unfeeling toward Southern people, but he was callous to the suffering of his own soldiers in prison, and to the loss of life on the battlefield. The President was the actor in building the fires. Not a spark of kindness or of humanity was in his heart.

And thus it came about that the 4th of July is not only notable as the day on which Independence was declared, but the day that President Lincoln informed Congress and the world that he had ignored the Constitution and begun a war on the Southern States.

16. Abraham Lincoln, the Citizen

Lincoln was six feet four inches tall, and while his body was of ordinary length his legs were very long, making him an odd figure. The circumstances of his life had been such that he had no natural affection for others, so his thoughts centered in himself.

His law partner, Herndon, says that Lincoln had no religion. Indeed there is a story told:

Mr. Lincoln was a candidate for Congress. One Sunday he went to church. The minister was very earnest in his sermon, and finally asked, "All who wish to go to Heaven to stand up." All stood up except Mr. Lincoln. The minister asked, "Mr. Lincoln, where do you wish to go?" Mr. Lincoln replied, "I wish to go to Congress." And Mr. Lincoln had his wish, for in 1847 he was elected to Congress.

In 1776, the several Colonies united in a Declaration of Independence; and in 1781 they entered into a Confederation.

Article 2 was: "Each State retains its sovereignty, freedom and independence and every power and right which is not by this Confederation expressly delegated to the United States in Congress assembled." Congress had such power as had been delegated to it by the States. Two years later Great Britain acknowledged the independence of every State, mentioning each by its name, "as free, sovereign and independent."

The Articles of Confederation contained a declaration that "the Union was to be perpetual" and in the same instrument the delegates solemnly "plighted and engaged the faith of their respective constituents that the Articles thereof shall be inviolately observed."

Now how did they treat these engagements? In 1787-less than six years later-eleven States deliberately discarded the Articles without asking two of them any odds, and adopted a new set of Articles of Union, but, instead of pronouncing the new Union "perpetual," they spoke of it as "a more perfect Union." By the use of these words they referred to an organization more perfect in its work and operation, as in time nothing can be more perfect than the "perpetuity" of the Articles.

Nothing was said in this new Constitution about a surrender of "the sovereignty, freedom and independence of the States," mentioned in the Articles, and there was a provision which really protected them. This provision read "the powers not delegated to the United States by the Constitution, nor prohibited by it to the States are reserved to the States respectively or to the people." Two of the eleven States, Virginia and New York, actually reserved the right of

withdrawing from the new Union at any time they deemed their rights violated. That is just what they had done with regard to the Union of 1781.

The eleven States that ratified this new Union selected Washington as President, and Congress met and passed laws. But these laws did not apply to Rhode Island nor to North Carolina which had declined to ratify the new instrument of government. After a year or more these two States joined the eleven and ratified the new Constitution, but Rhode Island made the same reservation as Virginia and New York. Then for the first time at the second session of the first Congress that body passed acts giving effect to its laws within the States of North Carolina and Rhode Island. It was understood that the people of every State had the right to have the government they would, just as was said in the Declaration of Independence a few years before.

Later Judge William Rawle, an honored citizen of Pennsylvania, in his book, A View of the Constitution, said explicitly, "The secession of a State depends on the will of the people of such a State." And that book was taught as a text at West Point.

Lodge, United States Senator from Massachusetts, says in his Life of Daniel Webster. "It is safe to say, that there was not a single man who did not regard the new system as an experiment from which every State had a right peaceably to withdraw."

In 1847 Abraham Lincoln was a member of Congress and took his oath to support the Constitution. On Jan. 12, 1848 he made a speech in Congress, in which he said, "Any people anywhere, being inclined, and having the power, have the right to rise up and shake off the existing government, and form a new one that suits them better."

When after years of battle President Davis sought to bring about peace and asked that President Lincoln would stop the fighting and let the people of each Southern State return the State into the Union, President Lincoln said: "No, let the Southern people stop fighting and submit to me." He would not let them return to the Union, for he held that they had never been out of the Union. He required that they submit to him. And in conformity with this demand is this sentence in his Inaugural a month later:

Yet, if God wills it that it continue until all the wealth piled by the bondsman's two hundred and fifty years of unrequited toil shall be sunk, until every drop of blood drawn with the lash shall be paid by another drawn with the sword as was said three thousand years ago, still it must be said: "The judgments of the Lord are true and righteous altogether."

In his so called amnesty proclamation he excepted from his mercy everybody of any importance in the South. In his second Inaugural he said: "If God wills that the war shall continue till every drop of blood drawn with the lash shall be paid by another drawn by the sword, etc." Where was the charity in this message? It is to be regretted that a President of the United States should have such a record. I doubt if Mr. Lincoln ever knew of a drop of blood coming from a Negro by the whipping of his master.

There is this historical incident. On Sept. 29, 1865, there was a convention of the Negroes of North Carolina at Raleigh, at which there was no White man. This convention declared: "Born upon the same soil and brought up in an intimacy of relationship, unknown to any other state of Society, we have formed attachment for the White race which must be as enduring as life We

have always loved our homes—now that freedom and a new career are before us, we love this land and people more than ever." Whipping for misdemeanors was usual and legal in all the States before the 60s and it is doubtful whether there were not more Whites whipped by the Sheriff than Negroes by their masters.

So Lincoln attributed the continuance of the war to the will of God. Yes, the Creator permitted it; and then presently there seems to have been a punishment. Did the Creator permit the life of Mr. Lincoln to be taken? With the facts stated how can it be doubted that the South was goaded into secession?

Lee having surrendered. General Johnston, likewise, surrendered, and the long war was over. Then the hell of hate, of which Caleb Cushing has spoken, glutted itself in Reconstruction. But if the doctrine of self-government proclaimed by Jefferson in the Declaration of Independence ever had any meaning, how could it ever have had a more complete application than it had in the case of the South?

"An abiding interest will always attach to the greatest war of modern times," says Historian Ellis (Vol. V, p. 266), 2,326,168 men of the North and 750,000 Southerners took part in the struggle. Of these, according to Fox's estimates in the Photographic History, Vol. X, the North lost 259,528 men killed in the field and died of wounds and disease, and the South lost 135,000 all told. In this stupendous conflict, therefore, the loss aggregated nearly half a million lives lost and mined in the armies, and even a greater number of Negro lives caused by neglect, disease and starvation, making a total of upwards of a million human lives. Not only this but the women and children on both sides suffered miseries. Then at the South there was desolation and min and poverty estimated in the long run at twenty billions of dollars.

The war was unnecessary. Lincoln could have averted it. Emancipation might have been delayed, but would have come in the natural course of events, without the loss of a single man or a single dollar. With the North calling the South all kinds of names the question could not be calmly considered in 1861.

This unnecessary war was Lincoln's real gift to posterity, his contribution as a citizen—all else was accidental. So Mr. Lincoln stands in history as one who did more evil than any man known to the world.

At the election in 1860 Abraham Lincoln was voted for by many of the Northern people who stood by John Brown and Negro insurrections and to whom Mr. Lincoln had given $ 100—and so it happened he was elected President—he was in line with Brown and Helper. (See Ashe's North Carolina History, Vol. XI, pp. 525-543).

It was thought that as President he would not stand by the Constitution, which not only protected Negro slavery at the South, but debarred Congress from preventing the importation of slaves for twenty years—that he was a dangerous man and would tolerate Negro insurrection. Therefore the people of South Carolina thought it best to escape Negro insurrections by leaving the Union. Then six other States followed that example. So it was a personal matter with Abraham Lincoln and he determined to start a war to keep the Southern States in the Union. In his Inaugural he sought to lay the blame for the war with the new Confederacy.

17. Lincoln the Strategist

While July, 1863, is commonly deemed the high-water mark of the Confederacy, apparently the summer of 1864 may be considered the low-water mark of the Northern States. In a general way it has been known that the opposition to Mr. Lincoln in Republican circles at that period made his renomination uncertain, but the reason for that opposition has not been clear. The following extract from an article entitled "Lincoln as a Strategist," contributed to the Forum, February, 1926, by Sir Frederick Maurice, incidentally presents a picture that is in a measure new and may be of interest to readers of the Veteran. This English writer says:

The slow and bloody progress through Virginia to the James, the failure of the first assaults on Lee's lines around Petersburg, the appearance of Early before the gates of the capital, produced a greater sense of disillusionment and of disappointment than had followed Burnside's repulse at Fredericksburg or Hooker's failure at Chancellorsville. The New York World, which had been exceptionally friendly to the commander in chief, asked on July 11: "Who shall revive the withered hopes that bloomed on the opening of Grant's campaign?" And nine days before Congress had invited the President to appoint a day for national prayer and humiliation. Horace Greeley attempted to open negotiations for peace by meeting Confederate commissioners at Niagara, and in the middle of July two other semiofficial seekers for peace, James F. Jacques and J.R. Gilmour, had gone to Richmond, only to be told by the Southern President: "If your papers tell the truth, it is your capital that is in danger, not ours.

In a military view I should certainly say our position is better than yours.' Greeley, despite the failure of his journey to Niagara, resumed his efforts to end the war, and on August 9th, wrote to the President: "Nine-tenths of the whole American people. North and South, are anxious for peace—peace on almost any terms—and utterly sick of human slaughter and devastation. I beg you, implore you, to inaugurate or invite proposals for peace forthwith. And, in case peace cannot now be made, consent to an armistice of one year, each party to retain unmolested all it now holds, but the rebel ports to be opened."

Not only was there this pressure from outside; there was discord within. Chase had resigned, a presidential election was drawing near, and there were outspoken predictions of a Republican defeat. The North was feeling as it had never felt before the strain of a prolonged conflict, and the nerves of even the most constant were atwitter, while, as a culmination of Lincoln's political perplexities, the rumblings of opposition to the draft, which had just become law, were growing daily louder. If ever a harassed statesman was justified in asking his generals to do something which would help him in his political trials, surely Lincoln would have been justified in so doing in August, 1864.

But what happened? Early in August the grumblings against the draft had alarmed Halleck, and on the eleventh of that month he told Grant: "Pretty strong evidence is accumulating that there is a combination formed, or forming, to make a forcible resistance to the draft in New York, Pennsylvania, Indiana, Kentucky, and perhaps some of the other States. The draft must be enforced, for otherwise the army cannot be kept up. But to enforce it may require the withdrawal of a considerable number of troops from the field. This possible, and I think very probable, exigency must be provided for." Four days later, on the evening of August 15, Grant answered from the lines before Petersburg: "If there is any danger of an uprising in the North to resist the draft, or for any other purpose, our loyal governors ought to organize the militia at once to resist it. If we are to draw troops from the field to keep the loyal States in harness, it will prove difficult to suppress the rebellion in the disloyal States. My withdrawal from the James River would mean the defeat of Sherman."

18. Conditions Just After the War

The following gives part of a letter written by Zebulon B. Vance just after the War between the States, to his friend, John Evans Brown, then in Sidney, New South Wales, Australia, and gives such a vivid picture of conditions at the time that it is a valuable record of those dark days. That General Vance did not follow the inclination to escape from the ills of which he wrote so feelingly was a fortunate thing for the South in view of the service he rendered in the restoration of his State as a part of the South. The letter was recently reproduced in the Raleigh News and Observer, a clipping of which was sent to the Veteran by Captain S. A. Ashe. The letter is as follows:

Of course I cannot give you much criticism upon the war, or the causes of our failure; nor can I attempt to do justice to the heroism of our troops or of the great men developed by the contest. This is the business of the historian, and when he traces the lines which are to render immortal the deeds of this revolution, if truth and candor guide his pen, neither our generals nor soldiers will be found inferior to any who have fought and bled within a century.

When all of our troops had laid down their arms, then was immediately seen the results which I had prophesied. Slavery was declared abolished—two thousand millions of property gone from the South at one blow, leaving four million freed vagabonds among us—outnumbering in several States the Whites—to hang as an incubus upon us and re-enact from time to time the horrors of Hayti and San Domingo. This alone was a blow from which the South will not with reasonable industry recover in one hundred years. Then too, the States have been reduced to the condition of territories, their executive and judicial (and all other) officers appointed by the Federal Government, and are denied all law except that of the military. Our currency, of course, is gone, and with it went the banks and bonds of the State, and with them went to ruin thousands of widows, orphans, and helpless persons whose funds were invested therein. Their railroads destroyed, towns and villages burned to ashes, fields and farm laid desolate, homes and homesteads, palaces and cabins only marked to the owner's eye by the blackened chimneys looming out on the landscape, like the mile-marks on the great highway of desolation as it swept over the blooming plains and happy valleys of our once prosperous land. The stock all driven off and destroyed, mills and agricultural implements specially ruined; many wealthy farmers making with their own hands a small and scanty crop with old artillery horses turned out by the troops to die.

This is but a faint picture of the ruin of the country which ten years ago you left blooming like the garden of Eden, abounding in plenty and filled with a population whose condition was the praise and the envy of all the earth! Alas, alas! To travel from New Bern to Buncombe now would cause you many tears, John, unless your heart is harder than I think it is. But, thank God,

though witchcraft and poverty doth abound, yet charity and brotherly love doth much more abound. A feeling of common suffering has united the hearts of our people and they help one another. Our people do not uselessly repine over their ruined hopes. They have gone to work with amazing alacrity and spirit. Major Generals, Brigadiers, Congressmen, and high functionaries hold the plough and sweat for their bread. A fair crop was the reward of last season's labor, and there will hardly be any suffering for next year except among the Negroes, who, forsaking their old masters, have mostly flocked into town in search of their freedom, where they are dying and will die by thousands. Trade begins feebly to resume its channels, and a beam of hope begins again to reanimate our long tried and suffering people. Our loss in men was very great. Seven-tenths of the spirited, educated young men of North Carolina fell in this struggle..

But I have dwelt long enough perhaps on this. After the surrender, I came to this place where Mrs. Vance had fled when Raleigh was evacuated, and sat down. In a few days I was arrested, sent to Washington City and lodged in prison. I remained there only two months when Mr. President permitted me to return home on parole. So I am here, a prisoner still. Mrs. Vance, during my confinement, was seized with hemorrhage of the lungs and came near dying. She is now, however, after much suffering, mental and bodily, restored to her usual health. We are living very poorly and quietly, as I can do no business until I am pardoned or released from my parole. We have four little boys, Charles (10 years old), David (8), Zebby (3), and Thomas (3). The two oldest go to school, are studying geography, etc., and keep in excellent health, though trouble and anxiety have left their marks on me. I am getting very gray.

There are indications that the radical abolitionists—the South being excluded from representatives in Congress—intend to force perfect Negro equality upon us. The right to vote, hold office, testify in courts and sit upon juries are the privileges claimed for them. Should this be done, and there is nothing to prevent it, it will revive an already half formed determination in me to leave the United States forever. Where shall I go? Many thoughts have I directed towards the distant Orient where you are. The idea is so possible at the least that I would be thankful to you for any information germain to the matter. Climate, soil, watercourses, government, population, etc., are all eagerly enquired after here. What could I do there—either in Australia or New Zealand -as a lawyer, grazier, merchant, or what not? What would it cost me and how would I go to get there? What could I do when set down at the wharf at Sidney with a wife, four children, and perhaps "nary red"? Tell me all about it. Should these things happen which we fear, my brother Robert (who was a Brigadier in the Southern Army) and I will go somewhere. At present there seems to be no prospect in the stability of the Government in Mexico, or vast numbers of our people would go there. Such a lot have gone anyhow..

When released from my bonds, I think of going to Wilmington, N.C., to practice law if I don't leave the country. The mountains were much torn and distracted by the war, being almost the only part of the State which was not thoroughly united. The state of society there is not pleasant, and I don't think I shall ever return there to live. Murder and outrage are frequent, and the absence of civil law encourages the wickedly inclined.

With every wish and sincerest prayers for your health, happiness, and prosperity in your new and distant home, believe me, my dear John, most faithfully and unchangeably,

Your devoted friend, Zebulon B. Vance

19. The War Between the Northern States and the Southern States

Secession began when South Carolina, in December, 1860, withdrew from the Union. The other Cotton States followed her example.

Congress was in session and made no protest. Members of Congress, on leaving their seats, made farewell speeches, shook hands with the other members, and returned to their States that claimed to be no longer in the Union but foreign States.

As they made these farewell addresses, Congress did not declare those men rebels, nor the inhabitants of these States to be in insurrection.

Months passed, and in March, President Lincoln declared that a State could not withdraw from the Union, and that all the inhabitants of the seceding States remained citizens of the United States, and all who obeyed their States were in insurrection.

Congress had not so declared, but Lincoln took steps to inaugurate a war and called on the States to furnish troops. The Northern States furnished troops.

At the December term of 1862 cases involving the legality of the blockade of the Southern ports were heard by the Supreme Court. In one of these cases, U. S. Reports, Volume 67, Justice Grier, on page 668, delivering the opinion of the court, said:

By the Constitution Congress alone has the power to declare a national or foreign war. It cannot declare war against a State or any number of States by virtue of any clause in the Constitution.

The President has no power to initiate or declare war against a foreign nation, or a domestic State.

But by act of 3rd of March, 1807, he can use the military forces and call out the militia to suppress insurrection.

Later on Justice Grier says:

We have shown that a civil war, such as that now waged between the Northern States and the Southern States, is properly conducted according to the humane regulations of public law, as regards captures on the ocean.

Under the very peculiar Constitution of this government, although the citizens owe supreme allegiance to the Federal Government, they owe also a qualified allegiance to the State in which they are domiciled. Their persons and property are subject to its laws. Hence in organizing this rebellion, they acted as States, claiming to be sovereign over all persons and property within their respective limits, and asserting a right to absolve their citizens from their allegiance to the Federal Government. Several of these States have combined to form a new Confederacy, claiming to be acknowledged by the world as a Sovereign State.

Their right to do so is now being decided by wager of Battle.

The above is a candid statement of the claims of the Northern and Southern States: that the Federal Government had no right under the Constitution to make war on a State; that the war was by the Northern States, and not by the Congress of the United States, under the Constitution.

It is to be observed that the court mentions that the claim of the North was that the inhabitants of each State owned a supreme allegiance to the Federal Government, but it naturally omits to state on what that claim was founded, for there is no such provision in the Constitution; and, indeed, several of the States in ratifying the Constitution, New York among them, particularly declared to the contrary, and no one of them asserted it, and says the court: "The right is now being decided by wager of battle"—not by law, the Constitution, and justice, but by force of arms!

conquest! And the conquest was not by the Federal Government under the Constitution, but by the Northern States.

While there was much to deplore after the war, yet the people of the South bowed their heads and accepted the situation. The following address of President Jefferson Davis well indicates the general spirit of the Southern leaders.

20. Speech of Jefferson Davis at Mississippi City, Mississippi in 1888

Mr. Chairman and Fellow Citizens:

Ah, pardon me, the laws of the United States no longer permit me to designate you as fellow citizens, but I am thankful that I may address you as my friends. I feel no regret that I stand before you this afternoon a man without a country, for my ambition lies buried in the grave of the Confederacy. There has been consigned not only my ambition, but the dogmas upon which that Government was based. The faces I see before me are those of young men; had I not known this I would not have appeared before you. Men in whose hands the destinies of our Southland lie, for love of her I break my silence, to speak to you a few words of respectful admonition. The past is dead; let it buzzier its dead, its hopes and its aspirations; before you lies the future—a future full of golden promise; a future of expanding national glory, before which all the world shall stand amazed. Let me beseech you to lay aside all rancor, all bitter sectional feeling, and to make your places in the ranks of those who will bring about a consummation devoutly to be wished—a reunited country.

General Lee and all other Southerners put into practice in their daily lives the thoughts President Davis professed in the above speech.